Personal Evangelism

A. P. Gibbs

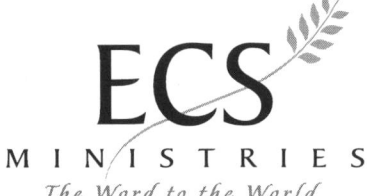
ECS
MINISTRIES
The Word to the World

Many ECS publications are also available in eBook formats.
For more information, visit our website www.ecsministries.org.

Personal Evangelism

Alfred P. Gibbs

Published by:

    ECS Ministries
    PO Box 1028
    Dubuque, IA 52004-1028
    phone: (563) 585-2070
    email: ecsorders@ecsministries.org
    website: www.ecsministries.org

First ECS Edition 2014
Reprinted 2016
ISBN 978-1-59387-220-5
Code: W-PE

Copyright © 1950, 1973, 2004, 2014 ECS Ministries

All rights reserved. No part of this publication may be reproduced or transmitted in any manner, electronic or mechanical, including photocopy, recording, or any information storage and retrieval system including the Internet without written permission from the publisher. Permission is not needed for brief quotations embodied in critical articles and reviews.

All Scripture quotations, unless otherwise indicated, are taken from the King James Version. Scripture marked RV indicated Revised Version.

Printed in the United States of America

Contents

Introduction		5
Chapter 1	The Need	7
Chapter 2	The Task	15
Chapter 3	Requirements	25
Chapter 4	More Requirements	33
Chapter 5	Hindrances	41
Chapter 6	Types of Sinner	47
Chapter 7	Methods in General	55
Chapter 8	The Right Approach	65
Chapter 9	The Careless and the Deceived	71
Chapter 10	Dealing with Delusion and "Churchianity"	79
Chapter 11	The Objector and the Skeptic	91
Chapter 12	More Types to Deal With	99

Introduction

Every time we meet Andrew in the New Testament, he is pointing someone to Christ. The first time we see him as a personal worker, bringing his own brother Simon to the Savior (John 1:40-41). What a great day that was in the annals of heaven! The second time we see him he is doing children's evangelism and is bringing a boy to the Lord Jesus (John 6:8-9). The third time he is engaged in foreign missionary work and is introducing certain Greeks to the Master (John 12:20-23). On each occasion Andrew is engaged in personal evangelism. Andrew seems to have been a firm believer in the maxim "hand-picked fruit is best."

This book is designed to help you equip yourself for the greatest of all ministries, that of bringing men and women, boys and girls to Christ. To help you understand the task, many Scripture references are given. Be sure to look them all up in your Bible. In each chapter there are eight verses to memorize. If you are serious about becoming a soul winner, you will not only memorize these verses, but many more as well. Another good idea would be to underline these verses in your Bible. You will find scores of verses in this book worth adding to your list of verses to memorize. The more Scripture you have at your fingertips, the more confidence you will have in speaking to men and women about their spiritual needs.

Chapter 1

The Need

There can surely be no doubt as to the tremendous importance of this subject of personal evangelism; and of its lack there can also be no question. One of the greatest needs today is for an army of Christian men and women, of all ages, "whose hearts God has touched" (1 Samuel 10:26), and upon whom He has laid the burden of winning souls for Christ by individual effort, and who are prepared to give themselves to the task of personal evangelism, cost what it may in time, money, effort, and prestige. There is not so much the need for public preachers and teachers, as there is for *personal workers*, who will make it their life's ambition to lead the lost to a saving and satisfying knowledge of the Son of God, Whom to know is life eternal (John 17:3).

Some Testimonies

J. G. Bellett, author of *The Moral Glory of the Lord Jesus Christ,* as he neared the end of his life said, "If I had my life to live over again, I would spend it in Sychar ministry." By this he meant that individual work which our Savior did with that woman by the side of the well of Sychar (John 4).

Think of the thousands of souls who have been led to Christ, not because they heard some famous and greatly-used evangelist, but through the self-sacrificing efforts of some lowly, godly and faithful soul winners who sought, unobtrusively, tactfully, and lovingly, to lead them to Christ. Perhaps the reader of these words is one of such. If so, then heed the message of the Savior, "Go thou and do likewise."

C.H. Spurgeon, "the prince of preachers," said, "Even if I were utterly selfish, and had no care for anything but my own happiness, I would choose, if I might, under God, to be a soul winner; for never did I know perfect, overflowing, unutterable happiness of the purest and most ennobling order, till I first heard of one who had sought and found the Savior through my means. No young mother ever so rejoiced over her first born child; no warrior was so exultant over a hard won victory!" Despite this glowing testimony, comparatively few seem to care to experience this "perfect, overflowing, and unutterable happiness."

Dr. R. A. Torrey also testified to the same experience, and declared he knew little of the joy of salvation until he had led his first soul to Christ. Truly, there is no joy comparable to soul winning!

Recommended Reading

The following excellent books on personal evangelism are warmly commended. They are listed in the order of their importance and value. Some of them are out of print, but can be secured from second-hand book stores. The fifth one named is particularly good. The student would be well advised to secure as many of these books as opportunity affords:

How to Bring Men to Christ	—R. A. Torrey
The Soul Winner	—C. H. Spurgeon
Lifestyle Evangelism	—J. Aldrich
How to Give Away Your Faith	—P. Little
Evangelism as a Lifestyle	—J. Petersen
Lost Art of Disciple Making	—L. Eims
Multiplying Disciples	—W. Moor
Born to Reproduce	—D. Trotman
Loving One Another	—G. Getz
Say It with Love	—H. Hendrichs
Out of the Saltshaker and into the World	—R. Pippert

Reading good gospel tracts will furnish the soul winner with a host of illustrations he can use in dealing with souls. Information as to methods of approach, the art of skillful questioning, and how to meet objections can be stored up in the memory, or noted in one's Bible alongside the Scripture to be used when the opportunity presents itself. However, it is not so much the reading of these books and tracts, or even the study of this course, but the *actual doing of it* that will produce the desired results, and make us the soul winners God desires us to be.

Practical Suggestions

To get the greatest benefit from this book, several things are essential.

1. *Supplication* at the throne of grace for a receptive and obedient heart to all the truth of the Word of God is vital. We need to pray for that illumination of mind and wisdom of spirit that only God can give; and which He delights to bestow in answer to the prayer of faith. See James 1:5-7.

2. *Concentration* in our study of the subject is important. This is not easy. The tendency of most people is to start with a burst of enthusiasm that promises much; but which is gradually allowed to cool off, until the subject is neglected, and finally abandoned. Remembering the words of James, "Behold, we count them happy which *endure*" (James 5:11, compare 1 Corinthians 15:58).

3. *Memorization* of the Scripture passages indicated is essential. You will sometimes be tested on these in this course. There is no easy road to memorization. The only way to commit verses of Scripture to memory is to *memorize* them! One good method is to get a quantity of good quality blank visiting cards, 5" x 3". On one side write the *location* of the verse to be memorized, say, "Romans 10:9-10." On the other side, write out, in full, the verse or verses to be memorized. Read these verses over and over, until you have thoroughly familiarized yourself with their exact wording. Soon you will have quite a number of these cards filled out. As you go from place to place, take out these cards. First look at the *location,* and see if you can repeat correctly the Scripture verses. When you have gone through them and repeated these without a mistake, reverse the process and look at the *Scripture* and see if you can give its location. (Use a Bible translation that is accurate and you are comfortable with.)

By means of *constant review,* these Scriptures will become part and parcel of you. Thus, saturated with the Scriptures, you will become expert in the use of "the sword of the Spirit, which is the word of God" (Ephesians 6:17). Remember, it is the Word of God, applied by the Spirit of God, that produces conviction of sin, generates faith in the hearer, and produces the new birth (John 16:7-13; Romans 10:17; James 1:18; 1 Peter 1:23).

In view of this, turn to each Scripture referred to in the text; read it carefully and prayerfully; mark it in your Bible and, if possible, memorize it. In any case follow the procedure outlined above for Romans 10:9-10.

This is no easy task, to be entered upon lightly, or laid aside carelessly. Increased light brings increased responsibility. It is better not to know, than to know and not to do. David said, "Neither will I offer . . . to the Lord . . . that which cost me nothing" (2 Samuel 24:24). What cost us nothing in effort is worth to us what it costs!

4. *Application* is essential. The value of this book depends on the measure in which these principles governing soul winning are individually *applied* and *practiced*. The measure of its *impression* on our hearts is determined by the degree of the *expression* in our lives. An old hymn sums it up thus:

"Still on Thy holy word
   We'd live, and feed, and grow;
Go on to know the Lord,
   And to practice what we know."

The Task Defined

By the expression "personal evangelism" is meant the attempt on the part of a Christian to show to another person, from the Word of God (1) his need, as a lost and guilty sinner, of a Savior and of God's salvation; (2) that Christ, the Son of God, is the Savior that he needs; (3) how to make Christ his own personal Savior; (4) what it involves to acknowledge Christ henceforth as the Lord of his life; and (5) how his inquiries, difficulties and objections are answered in the Word of God. Each Christian worker must, in view of this, have Paul's motto as his: "I am made all things unto all men, that I might by all means save some" (1 Corinthians 9:22; compare Proverbs 11:30).

Here are five questions to ask yourself, solemnly and sincerely, in God's presence:
1. Do I really believe that God wants to save men? (1 Timothy 2:3-4).
2. Do I believe that God can save men, instantly and completely, through human instrumentality? (Acts 15:7; 1 Peter 1:23-25; Acts 8:35-37).
3. Do I believe that God *can* use me? Am I really saved and assured of my own salvation?
4. Do I believe that God *will* use me?
5. Am I *willing* to let God use me?

Years ago D. L. Moody heard Henry Varley say, "The world has yet to see what God can do with a man who is wholly yielded to Him." He determined that, by the grace of God, he would be that man, and the effect of his devoted life to Christ bears eloquent testimony to the truth of Varley's statement (Romans 12:1, 2; 6:13; 1 Corinthians 6:19-20; Acts 20:24; Philippians 1:20-21). For D. L. Moody was used of God in two continents. Thousands were saved through his preaching and the influence of his life is still felt in the world through the great institutions he founded.

As our lives are thus yielded to Him we can then truthfully pray:

> "Lord, lay some soul upon my heart,
>   And love that soul through me;
> And may I truly do my part,
>   To bring that soul to Thee."

Verses to Memorize

Thou shalt not make unto thee any graven image, or any likeness of anything that is in heaven above, or that is in the earth beneath, or that is in the water under the earth. Thou shalt not bow down thyself to them, nor serve them: for I the Lord thy God am a jealous God, visiting the iniquity of the fathers upon the children unto the third and fourth generation of them that hate me.	He, that being often reproved hardeneth his neck, shall suddenly be destroyed, and that without remedy.
This book of the law shall not depart out of thy mouth; but thou shalt meditate therein day and night, that thou mayest observe to do according to all that is written therein: for then thou shalt make thy way prosperous, and then thou shalt have good success.	The fear of man bringeth a snare: but whoso putteth his trust in the Lord shall be safe.
And if it seem evil unto you to serve the Lord, choose you this day whom ye will serve; whether the gods which your fathers served that were on the other side of the flood, or the gods of the Amorites, in whose hand ye dwell: but as for me and my house, we will serve the Lord.	Come now, and let us reason together, saith the Lord: though your sins be as scarlet, they shall be as white as snow; though they be red like crimson, they shall be as wool.
Boast not thyself of tomorrow; for thou knowest not what a day may bring forth.	To the law and to the testimony: if they speak not according to this word, it is because there is no light in them.

Proverbs 29:1	Exodus 20:4-5
Proverbs 29:5	Joshua 1:8
Isaiah 1:18	Joshua 24:15
Isaiah 8:20	Proverbs 27:1

Chapter 2

The Task

We shall notice seven reasons for the importance of this work of personal evangelism.

Scripture Endorses It

1. God Himself Desires It

God proves this by the revelation of His name. God's name predicates His character. God speaks of Himself as *"Savior"* seven times in the Old Testament. Look up these references: Psalm 106:21; Isaiah 43:3; 45:15; 45:21; 49:26; 60:16; 63:8. The same title is given to God in the New Testament (Luke 1:47; 1 Timothy 1:1; 4:10; Titus 1:3; 2:10; Jude 25).

It is the desire of His heart (Ezekiel 33:11; 18:23, 32; Hosea 11:8; 1 Timothy 2:4; 2 Peter 3:9).

In sending His Son, God proves His desire for the salvation of men. Christ came, not *in order* that God might love us, but *because* God loved us (1 John 4:14; Galatians 4:4; Acts 3:26; John 3:16-17). Thus the great God Himself is intensely concerned with the salvation of sinners.

2. Christ Revealed It

He did this first by His own example. He knew He had $3^1/_2$ to 4 years of public ministry, yet He did not neglect personal work. He chose His disciples *individually* (Mark 3:14; 1:16; John 1:43; Matthew 4:21-22; 9:9). He engaged in *personal* conversations. See John 3; 4; 5:1-9; 9; Luke 10:38; 7:36-50; 23:39-43; etc. The great truths of the new birth and worship were revealed to individuals.

His own command to and commission of His disciples reveals Christ's passion for the souls of men (Mark 16:15-16; Matthew 28:19-20). Note the four "alls" of Matthew 28:19-20. One speaks of His *power;* one of the *parish:* "all nations," one of His *program:* "teach all things," and one of His *presence:* "with you all the days." In Mark 1:17 is an *invitation,* "come," an *obligation,* "follow," a *contemplation,* "Me," and an *occupation,* "fishers of men." See the margin of Luke 5:10 in the Revised Version. It reads, "Take men alive." Compare this with 2 Timothy 2:26. Here are two fishermen, Satan and the Christian, both seeking to "take men alive."

Consider Luke 8:39 and compare it with Mark 5:19. Here Christ commissions His disciple to show by his life and tell by his lips what Christ had done for him. Someone has said, "It is the double testimony of lip and life that convinces men and confounds demons." See also Acts 1:8. We are His witnesses to tell what we have seen, heard, and know of Him.

3. The Early Church Practiced It

At Pentecost all spake (Acts 2:4). Note the result in 2:41. See also Acts 3:1-9; 3:12; 4:8-12; 9:1-22; 8:35; 8:1 and compare these verses with Acts 11:19. God blessed this primitive method of "gossiping the gospel"; for we read "so mightily grew the word of God and prevailed" (Acts 19:20). Of the 112 times in the New Testament that the word "preach" is used, in only six instances does it mean a formal discourse.

4. The Church Today Cannot Exist without It

The Church that does not *go* with the gospel will soon be *gone!* The assembly that loses its evangelistic fervor, and settles down in smug self-complacency as "headquarters for the truth" will soon cease to exist. The Church in Jerusalem was *shattered* that it might be *scattered,* and all its members became personal evangelists (Acts 11:19).

The curse came upon the people of Meroz, not because of any wrong thing they did, but because of the right thing they failed to do. Instead of striving together with their brethren against the common enemy, they did nothing (Judges 5:23). The Christian who gives nothing to the Lord, and does nothing for the Lord is good for—nothing! The Lord deliver us from being good-for-nothing Christians!

It Is the Believer's Responsibility

Read, preferably on your knees and alone with God, Ezekiel 33:1-6; Proverbs 24:11-12; James 5:19-20; 1 Corinthians 9:16-27. Surely the believer should not need any more convincing, after reading these solemn truths, of the supreme importance and responsibility of soul winning.

Consider the following weighty words from the pen of T. C. Horton, "Soul winning is a Divine art. Men are not born soul winners, but made. Some Christians seem to think that only a few believers are called to this work, and that the obligation is not universal; that it may or may not be done as we choose. This is false, unscriptural and illogical. It is committed to every believer. All may become soul winners if they give themselves to it."

Dr. Nettleton, a great evangelist and soul winner, once put to himself the question, "What shall I wish I had done with my life a thousand years from now?" He answered his own question by devoting his life to the winning of souls for Christ.

Suppose you were offered $1,000.00 for every soul you earnestly sought to win for Christ. Would you, for this reward, seek to win more souls for Christ than you are doing right now? If so, your love for money is greater than your love for Christ or your fellow man!

It is said that Rome "conquered the world with the short sword." It enabled them to get at close grips with the enemy. In modern warfare it takes over a ton of steel to kill a man, and often a ton of sermons to convert one soul. This is not so with the "short sword" of personal dealing with individuals.

Judge Mingins in his youth had been an infidel in Philadelphia. He left that city and was converted to God. Sometime after his conversion he revisited Philadelphia, and stayed in the home of one of his old time infidel friends. After three days in his home his friend said, "George, I hear you're a Christian." "Yes," was his reply. "Well, George, you believe in God?" "Yes." "And in hell, and that all the impenitent will go there for all eternity?" "Yes." "Well, does Christianity dry up all the milk of humanity in one's body, as it has *yours*?" "What do you mean?" inquired the judge. "Well," said his friend, "you have lived three days under my roof, knowing and believing all this, and you have not put your hand on my shoulder, or said one word to save me!" Could the same be said of us?

Those Who Win Souls Are "Wise" (Proverbs 11:30)

The marginal reference of this verse reads, "taketh souls." What does it mean to "win" souls? Joseph Kemp points out that the word "win" is *a military term*. To win a city is to lay siege to it and take it. This is not easy work. It calls for skill, patience, bravery and endurance. To capture the city of Mansoul is indeed a great feat of arms. Each student should read Bunyan's "Holy War" to appreciate this fact. It is also *an occupational term*. To "take" a soul suggests a fisherman who, in the face of all kinds of weather and risks, applies himself to the task of pitting his skill against the fish to the cost of the latter. All disciples of Isaac Walton can readily appreciate this illustration. Moreover it is *a matrimonial term*. The way to win a bride is by captivating her affections. See how the bride was won for Isaac in Genesis 24. When a man pays court to a woman with the object of winning her as his bride, how does he go about it? He pays her attention; he calls on her; walks with her; talks with her; sends her presents; sacrifices his own ease and self interests in order to be with her; and finally places a proposition of marriage to her to which she answers "Yes." He has won her!

Now apply this to the winning of a soul to Christ, and you have a striking example of the path of true wisdom. Chadwick well says, "It is a noble work. There's nothing higher. Angels covet it. It is a lasting work, for its results are seen in eternity. It is a soul profiting work, for it makes for spiritual success, happiness and freshness."

The Value of the Soul

By the word "soul" is meant the spiritual part of man, as distinct from his body (Mark 8:36-37; Psalm 49:8; Matthew 10:28).

We compute the value of the soul in several ways.

1. Its Nature and Origin

Man was created by God and is a tripartite being (Genesis 2:7; 1 Thessalonians 5:23). Through his body he becomes *world* conscious, through his soul he becomes *self* conscious, and through his spirit he may become *God* conscious. It is this, the possession of a spirit, that distinguishes man from brute creation.

2. Its Capabilities and Powers

Man has a capacity for God, or for evil; fellowship with God, or service for the Devil; of being a blessing or a curse to his fellow man. O, the vast possibilities for good or evil in each soul!

3. Its Valuation by Christ

Calvary proclaims God's estimation of the value of the soul. The precious blood of Christ was shed to secure its redemption (1 Peter 1:18-19). Note Christ's own illustration (Matthew 13:44-46; compare Galatians 2:20).

4. Its Eternal Existence

The soul exists forever either in heaven, or the lake of fire (Mark 9:43-48). Christ taught this fact clearly (Luke 16:19-31; Matthew 10:28).

5. The Battle for Its Possession

The human soul is the battleground between God and the Devil (Luke 11:21-23). Christ's word "strive" means "agonize" (Luke 13:24-30). The soul winner is up against the Devil and his hordes (Ephesians 6:11-12).

Sir William Hamilton said, "There is nothing great on earth but man, and there is nothing great about man but his soul." The personal worker must see men, not so much as *bodies* having *souls;* but *souls* having *bodies.* He must bend every endeavor to win that soul for Christ. Worlds cannot compensate a person for the loss of his soul. A diamond digger endures all sorts of privations and untold hardships; but counts them well invested if he can but find one valuable gem. Who knows that we may be the means of winning a Moody or a Spurgeon for our blessed Lord?

The Fact of Eternity

Read Matthew 13:41-43, 49-51; 25:30-46. What shall we say about eternity? No human language can adequately describe it, or mind conceive it. The Poet has said:

> "Count the gold and silver blossoms
>   Spring has scattered o'er the lea;
> Count the softly winding ripples
>   Sparkling o'er the summer sea;
> Count the lightly flickering shadows
>   In the autumn forest glade;"
> Count the falling feathery snowflakes
>   Icy gems by winter made;
> Count the myriad blades that glitter
>   Early in the morning dew;

> Count the desert strand that stretches
>   Under noontide's vault of blue;
> Count the notes that wood birds warble
>   In the evening's fading light;
> Count the stars that gleam and twinkle
>   O'er the firmament by night . . .
> When thy counting all is done,
>   Scarce eternity's begun!
> Hearer, pause: "Where wilt thou be
>   During thy eternity?"

General Booth, founder of the Salvation Army, used to say that every Christian ought to be sent to hell for a week, for this would make a lost eternity so real to him he would spend the rest of his life on earth in seeking to deliver people from the possibility of eternal damnation. Finney, the famous evangelist, advised Christians to look, as though through a telescope, and see the misery of the lost and hear their groans; and then look to heaven and see the joys and hear the songs of the redeemed. Then each believer should ask, "Is it possible that I should so prevail with God as to be the means of elevating the lost sinner to that glorious place?"

An infidel once said, "If I truly, firmly, and consistently believed, as millions say they do, that the knowledge and practice of religion in this life influences destiny in another; religion should be to me everything. I would cast aside earthly enjoyments as dross, earthly cares as follies, and earthly thought and feelings as less than vanity. Religion would be my first waking thought, and my last image when sleep sunk me into unconsciousness." It was these words that stirred C. T. Studd to the depths, and sent him first to China, and then to Africa to burn out for Christ. Alexander Marshall, author of the greatly used booklet *God's Way of Salvation,* used to say, "A soul saved, saves that soul from more misery, anguish and torment than has ever been suffered by all the people of the world from the beginning of time, to this time, and from this time to the end of time; for that soul has been saved from *eternal* punishment. A soul saved brings that soul into possession of more joy, peace and blessing than has ever been enjoyed by all the people of God from the beginning of time until this time, and from this time until the end of time, for that soul has been brought into possession of *eternal* joy."

No wonder one earnest soul winner prayed, "Lord, stamp 'Eternity' on my eyeballs, that all I see, may be seen in the light of eternity!"

The Shortness of Time

Read John 9:4; Ephesians 5:14-16; 2 Corinthians 6:1-2; 2 Timothy 4:2, 3; Romans 13:11-12. Life's little day will soon draw to a close, and the time of our opportunity for service be gone forever.

A French philosopher said, "He who values his life must be careful of his time; for time is the stuff out of which life is made." Boreham said, "Just as space is a tabloid of infinity, so time is a tabloid of eternity." David Brainerd, missionary to the Indians, who died at the age of 36, wrote in his diary, "I wanted to wear myself out in His service for His glory. I cared not how or where I lived, or what hardships I went through, so that I could but gain souls for Christ."

Someone has said that Paul's concern for the lost was produced by a three-fold conviction. He was convinced of one great verity all must face: the judgment of God (Romans 14:10); of one great experience through which all must pass: the resurrection, either of life or condemnation; and of one great destiny toward which all men are moving: eternity.

The farmer who neglects to plow and sow his fields in the spring, must face the prospect of empty barns in the fall, unless he desires a harvest of weeds! Read Ecclesiastes 11:1-6.

How can we get this concern for souls, and learn to value rightly the opportunities that lie to our hand? It is only as we face the Word of God in the presence of God. Let us ponder prayerfully what is involved by the words: "condemned already"; "hath not life"; "lost"; and "perishing" (John 3:18; 1 John 5:12; 1 Corinthians 1:18).

God Honors Personal Work

Andrew is a picture of the personal worker. He is mentioned three times, and each time he is described as bringing someone to Christ (John 1:40-42; 6:8-9; 12:22).

We are faced today with a great deal of "professional" mass evangelism. With its high pressure methods it has manufactured thousands of false conversions. The great need is for consecrated Christians who will give themselves to the task of personal evangelism. One soul genuinely saved is better than ten thousand empty professions. Let us go in for *quality* and not quantity.

Trumbull, a great soul winner and author of *Taking Men Alive*, said, "I can talk to a multitude, and not see any moved; but I can talk to a multitude of individuals in the course of time and I can get a multitude of results." D. L. Moody said, "My sermon is but the preliminary to the individual work in the inquiry room." The Word of God gives us no authority to say, "Come ye from all the world and hear the gospel from our platform." Christ said, "Go ye into all the world and preach the gospel to every creature."

There is a vast difference between being evangelical and *evangelistic*. The former may be sound doctrinally and sound asleep at the same time. The evangelical serves the truth on ice; the evangelist gives the truth on fire. Let us not be like the Christian who, on his death bed, confessed, "I am saved and going to heaven, but I am going empty handed, without having won one soul for Christ my Savior."

It has been calculated that if 100 believers each brought one soul to Christ each year; and each soul won, in turn, brought another to Christ each year; in 25 years over a billion and a half souls would be saved! As it now is, the average conversion is about four a year for every hundred Christians, a poor showing. A proverb says, "You can count the acorns on a tree, but you cannot count the number of oak trees in an acorn,"—providing, of course, that the acorn dies (John 12:24).

The distinction between the preaching of a sermon and a personal effort is the same difference as a patent medicine "cure all," and the personal visit of the doctor. The doctor examines the patient, diagnoses the disease, and prescribes the remedy. Let us develop this ability for individual effort, and seek, by all the means at our command, to win souls by personal evangelism.

Verses to Memorize

I, even I, am he that blotteth out thy transgressions for mine own sake, and will not remember thy sins.	Yea, they have chosen their own ways, and their soul delighteth in their abominations. I also will choose their delusions, and will bring their fears upon them; because when I called, none did answer; when I spake, they did not hear; but they did evil before mine eyes, and chose that in which I delighted not.
Look unto me, and be ye saved, all the ends of the earth: for I am God, and there is none else.	For my people have committed two evils; they have forsaken me the fountain of living waters, and hewed them out cisterns, broken cisterns, that can hold no water.
But he was wounded for our transgressions, he was bruised for our iniquities: the chastisement of our peace was upon him; and with his stripes we are healed. All we like sheep have gone astray; we have turned everyone to his own way; and the Lord hath laid on him the iniquity of us all.	And she shall bring forth a son, and thou shalt call his name JESUS: for he shall save his people from their sins.
But the wicked are like the troubled sea, when it cannot rest, whose waters cast up mire and dirt. There is no peace, saith my God, to the wicked.	For I say unto you, That except your righteousness shall exceed the righteousness of the scribes and Pharisees, ye shall in no case enter into the kingdom of heaven.

Isaiah 6:3b-4	Isaiah 43:25
Jeremiah 2:3	Isaiah 45:22
Matthew 1:21	Isaiah 53:5-6
Matthew 5:20	Isaiah 57:20-21

Chapter 3

Requirements

As we consider the essential requirements for personal evangelism we assume that the person who engages in it has been regenerated by the Spirit of God.

Assurance of One's Own Salvation

We must "speak that which we know" (John 3:11). Supposing the person with whom you were dealing asked, "Are *you* certain that you are saved?" Could you reply with conviction, "Yes, thank God, I am!" Supposing he were next to inquire, "How do you know?" Could you point out to him that, relying on the finished work of Christ for you on the cross, and trusting Him as your own personal Savior made you perfectly *safe;* and that believing in the written Word of God made you absolutely *sure* (1 John 5:13)? Memorize this verse.

Paul could say, "Seeing we have such hope, we use great plainness [or boldness] of speech" (2 Corinthians 3:12). A firm conviction produces a plain confession which, in turn, encourages confidence on the part of the hearer (2 Corinthians 4:13). Make certain, from the Word of God, that you are truly saved through resting in the work of Christ alone for salvation, and in the Word of God alone for assurance.

Conviction That Men Are Lost without Christ

It is only as a doctor properly diagnoses the disease of the patient that he can correctly prescribe the remedy. The Word of God leaves no doubt about man's state by nature. Thoroughly familiarize yourself with the deep need of those to whom you witness.

1. The Unsaved Man Is Dead, Needing Regeneration

Read Ephesians 2:1-2; John 3:1-16. Death, in Scripture, means separation. *Physical* death is the separation of the spirit from the body (James 2:26). *Spiritual* death is the separation of the sinner from the life of God (Ephesians 4:18; 1 John 5:12; John 3:36). The *Second* death is the eternal fixation of this state of separation, body, soul, and spirit, from God (Revelation 20:12-15).

Death has been defined as, "The cessation of correspondence with environment" (see Genesis 2:17). Did Adam die the day he ate of the forbidden fruit? Yes. He did not die *physically* but *spiritually*. When Adam sinned, his correspondence with God ceased for he separated himself from Him. Thus he died spiritually. Now see Luke 15:24. When was the prodigal "dead"? While he was in the far country, separated from his father and having no correspondence with him. See also 1 Timothy 5:6.

Since man is spiritually *dead* to God, his great need is *life* from God. The communication of this life to a sinner is *regeneration* (i.e., the new birth). Memorize John 1:12-13. In this passage three popular misconceptions regarding the new birth are dealt with. It is not by heredity, or "not of blood." People do not have life in Christ because their parents were Christians. Spiritual life is not inherited. Each needs to be regenerated for himself. It is not by self effort, or "the will of the flesh." No person can regenerate himself, or produce his own birth; no more than he can produce his own physical birth. It is not by human instrumentality, or "of the will of man." Thousands are trusting to this and imagine that through baptism, confirmation, church membership or communion, they are introduced into this new birth. Scripture makes clear that no human will or action can produce it.

Then comes the great truth, "but of *God*." God alone is the source of this new birth. Man is helpless and lifeless. Only as God quickens him can he live (1 John 5:1). The Word of God is heeded with the hearing of faith; Christ is received as Savior; the believing sinner is sealed with the Spirit of God and thus he is regenerated (John 5:24-25; Galatians 3:2; John 1:12; Ephesians 1:13). Only *God* can regenerate. The overzealous personal worker sometimes tries to do what only God can do. We can put the Word of God clearly before the sinner; but we cannot awaken within him one anxious thought, or communicate to him the spiritual life he needs.

2. The Unsaved Man Is Lost, Needing Salvation

Study Luke 19:10; 2 Corinthians 4:3. The word "lost" can have two meanings. It can mean that a thing is not in the possession of its lawful owner or it can mean that a person is ignorant of his whereabouts, or how to find the way to his destination.

In Luke 15 the words "lost" and "lose" occur seven times. A threefold description of the lost sinner is given. The sheep was lost through *straying* (Luke 15:1-7 compare Isaiah 53:6). Man has a wayward nature, and must be sought and found if he is to be saved. The coin was lost through a *fall* and, though valuable, lay helpless to recover itself and had to be sought and found. The prodigal was lost through *willfulness*, "He took his journey," he did not wander, or fall. In self-will he squandered his resources, and he had to repent, resolve and return before he could be saved.

The sinner is "lost," and nothing short of salvation can meet his need. Salvation is the work of God which results in that which is lost being found or saved and only God can accomplish this work of salvation.

3. The Unsaved Man Is a Slave, Needing Redemption

The sinner is under the control, or in the possession of another. Sin is viewed as a master, and the sinner as its bondslave, helpless to deliver himself (John 8:34; Romans 6:16, 20; 7:14). Therefore he needs to be redeemed. Redemption is the act by which one frees a person or thing from the possession and power of another by the payment of the ransom price.

This world is a vast slave camp in which people are the slaves of lying, cursing, lust, passion, pride, covetousness, drink, fashion, pleasure, religion, and self, etc. How are they to be redeemed and set free from their bondage? They need to be brought into touch with Christ the Redeemer. He came to redeem (Luke 4:18; Mark 10:45). He paid the ransom price for their redemption (Galatians 3:13; 4:4-5; 1 Peter 1:18-19; 1 Corinthians 6:20). He ever lives to deliver from the bondage of sin each sinner who comes to Him (John 8:32, 36; Ephesians 1:7; Galatians 5:1). Deliverance from sin's penalty and power is found in a Person—and that Person is the Son of God.

4. The Unsaved Man Is Blind, Needing Illumination

Man, by nature, is blind to spiritual realities. His understanding is darkened (Ephesians 4:18). He is blinded by Satan (2 Corinthians 4:4). He cannot "see" the kingdom of God (John 3:3). He cannot receive or understand spiritual things (1 Corinthians 2:14). He dwells in darkness and loves it (John 1:5; Colossians 1:13; John 3:19). He needs to have his spiritual eyes opened (Acts 26:18).

Christ came to bring light (John 8:12; 9:5; Luke 4:18). His words enlighten us about God, sin, the sinner, salvation, the problems of life, the eternal bliss of the saved, and the doom of the Christ rejecter (Psalm 119:130).

All who trust Christ are brought into the light (2 Corinthians 4:6; Ephesians 5:8). Do not be surprised when an unsaved person says, "But I *can't,* or I don't *see* it this way." How can they see, unless their eyes are opened? The Scriptures, when applied by the Spirit of God, open the eyes of the sinner to the truth of his need, and of God's remedy.

5. The Unsaved Man Is a Rebel, Needing Reconciliation

Man is in a state of antagonism to God. He is at enmity with God, that is, he is hostile in his attitude to God (Romans 5:10; 8:7-8; Colossians 1:21, RV; Titus 3:3). He hates the truth, resents God's Word and refuses Christ His rightful place as Lord (Romans 1:20-21, 28; compare Daniel 5:23). The closing words of this verse are God's indictment of all humanity.

Man therefore requires reconciliation. He needs to be brought back to God in repentance and submission and become His loyal subject. Look at Luke 14:31-32. Soltau who wrote the book entitled *Personal Work For Christ*, sums up this verse thus, "Here is a king (the sinner) mustering his forces and taking counsel with himself as to how he, with his pitiful army of sins, thoughts, opinions, resolves, and purposes, under General Self-will, can meet God's twenty thousand holy requirements, purposes, and precepts. He therefore seeks conditions of reconciliation. They are simple. The sinner must own his rebellion, believe the gospel, surrender unconditionally to Christ, and thus come under the beneficent authority and Lordship of the One by whose blood the peace was made" (Colossians 1:20; 2 Corinthians 5:19-21).

6. The Unsaved Man Is a Criminal, Needing Justification

Sin is a crime against God and His moral government. Make yourself familiar with what the Word of God has to say on this subject.

Man is a sinner by nature. He was born possessed of a nature opposed to God (Psalm 51:5). This nature is called "the flesh," and loves all that which God hates, and hates that which God loves (Romans 8:5-9). A person does not have to sin in order to *become* a sinner; he sins because he *is* a sinner. The sinful nature is the *root*, of which his sinful words and deeds are the *fruit* (Mark 7:21-23; Jeremiah 17:9).

Man is a sinner by choice and practice. This sinful nature soon reveals itself in sinful thoughts entertained in the mind; sinful words that escape the lips; sinful deeds done in the life, and a sinful attitude adopted toward God. God gives a full length portrait of the sinner in Romans 3:10-19, 23, and each Christian worker should be well acquainted with this passage. All sin, whether directed against self or one's fellow men, is primarily against God Himself (Psalm 51:4). The enormity of a crime is determined by the one against whom it is committed, hence sin is a crime against God (Hosea 7:2; Amos 5:12; Titus 3:3; Romans 1:28-32; Psalm 14:2-3). Our sins of thought (Matthew 5:28), word (Matthew 12:34-37), and deed (Jeremiah 44:4; Proverbs 6:16) are hated by God and must be punished by God, either in the person of the sinner, or the sinner's Substitute, who bears his sins and dies in his stead.

Man's need is justification before God. To justify is to declare righteous. Justification is that act of God by which He declares the sinner, who trusts in the substitutionary sacrifice of His Son and receives Him as Savior and Lord, to be righteous in His sight. Thus it is more than pardon, for God views the believer as though he never had sinned at all! See Romans 3:24-26; 5:1-2; Galatians 2:16.

7. The Unsaved Man Is a Debtor Needing Pardon

The sinner is bankrupt, unable to pay his debt to God. Man owes God a life of obedience to His laws, honor to His name, and service in His cause. This he has failed to give (Luke 7:41-42). God has loaned man a life with all its possibilities, for which one day he must give account (Romans 14:12). Many falsely imagine they can pay their debt by issuing more and more promissory notes to live a better life in the future; but all such hopes are vain. Neither his good works, tears, prayers, religious exercises, nor good resolutions can pay the debt.

God has provided a pardon, a complete discharge from that debt, because of the work of His Son, who assumed our liability and paid it in full by His own precious blood (Isaiah 43:25; 44:22; 55:7; Acts 3:19; 13:38; Colossians 2:13; Micah 7:18-19).

As we view the sinner in the light of God's description we can surely appreciate his helpless and hopeless state. Only the mighty grace and power of God can reach and save him. This grace and power is revealed in the gospel that we must present to him, clearly and prayerfully.

You will observe that there are many Scriptures in this lesson which should be added to your growing collection of verses to be memorized. Be sure to put them on cards and plan to learn them by heart.

Verses to Memorize

Enter ye in at the strait gate: for wide is the gate, and broad is the way, that leadeth to destruction, and many there be which go in thereat: Because straight is the gate, and narrow is the way, which leadeth unto life, and few there be that find it.	For what shall it profit a man, if he shall gain the whole world, and lose his own soul?
But when Jesus heard that, he said unto them, They that be whole need not a physician, but they that are sick. But go ye and learn what that meaneth, I will have mercy, and not sacrifice: for I am not come to call the righteous, but sinners to repentance.	For the Son of man is come to seek and to save that which was lost.
Whosoever therefore shall confess me before men, him will I confess also before my Father which is in heaven.	But as many as received him, to them gave he power to become the sons of God, even to them that believe on his name: Which were born, not of blood, nor of the will of the flesh, nor of the will of man, but of God.
For out of the heart proceed evil thoughts, murders, adulteries, fornications, thefts, false witness, blasphemies: These are the things which defile a man: but to eat with unwashen hands defileth not a man.	Jesus answered and said unto him, Verily, verily, I say unto thee, Except a man be born again, he cannot see the kingdom of God.

Mark 8:36	Matthew 7:13-14
Luke 19:10	Matthew 9:12-13
John 1:12-13	Matthew 10:32
John 3:3	Matthew 15:19-20

Chapter 4

More Requirements

A Right Relationship with Christ

If we love Him, we will obey Him (John 14:15, 23; 15:10; 1 Corinthians 13:4-7; 2 Corinthians 5:14). God's love has been *shed* abroad in our hearts to be *spread* abroad from our hearts (Romans 5:5). Only as His love becomes the constraining motive for our service will that service become really worthwhile. Apart from love to Christ, service for Him will be a cold and perfunctory business. His love will then be not so much a "love that will not let me go," as a "love that will not let me stay" at home in ease while souls are perishing.

As the love of Christ was shown by His sacrifice for us, so our love for Christ is measured by the amount of sacrifice we make for Him. Christ loved us and gave Himself for us (Galatians 2:20). The least we can do is to give ourselves to Him and give ourselves wholeheartedly to the work that lies so near and dear to His heart—the salvation of the lost. The cost, in the shape of time, energy, prayer, study, and self-denial, will be well worthwhile for the day of rewards is coming (2 Timothy 4:4-8)!

A Knowledge of the Word of God (2 Timothy 2:15)

This is of great importance. You must acquire, as quickly as possible, a general and working knowledge of the Bible. Without this you cannot be much used of God. You must be convinced of the Divine inspiration, authority, and inerrancy of the Bible (2 Timothy 3:15-16). You must have no doubt about its authenticity, or its full inspiration. You must *study* it with steadfast and concentrated determination; *quote* it with earnest conviction, and *use* it with skill and discrimination. There are four reasons why.

The Word of God produces conviction of sin when applied to the conscience by the Spirit of God (Acts 2:37). It is a living word (Hebrews 4:12 "quick" = "alive," compare 2 Timothy 4:1). It both generates and sustains spiritual life. It speaks, pleads, argues, and answers every question. It is a seed that contains a life principle within itself (1 Peter 1:23). It is powerful, or energetic. Many have been saved through the text who never heard a word of the sermon (Romans 1:16; 1 Thessalonians 2:13). It is cutting. It is a sword (Ephesians 6:17). Use it, quote it, and let it do its work (Acts 7:54). Like a plow, it cuts into the soil of the heart and reveals what lies hidden beneath the surface. It pierces. It can reach down into the deep recesses of the heart and expose the "thoughts and intents." It is a "critic" that criticizes the sinner. It divides asunder. It separates between the soul and spirit, between the natural and the spiritual, between the saved and the unsaved, between the empty professor and the true possessor. It lays bare man's inmost secrets, hidden ambitions, self-will, lusts, and secretly cherished sin.

The Word of God reveals the way of salvation (2 Timothy 3:14-15). Use it when you deal with souls, for it both shows them their need of salvation and the salvation they need. It brings assurance of salvation (1 John 5:13). It is only a "thus saith the Lord" that brings assurance to a soul. It assures the believer of his salvation (Romans 10:9-10; John 5:24; 1 John 5:13), of his security (John 10:27-30; Romans 8:35-39), and of his future blessedness (John 14:1-3). Each soul should be anchored to the Word of God. Moreover it gives guidance for the life (Psalm 119:105, 130; Proverbs 6:20-24; 2 Peter 1:3-4). It gives light on every problem that may arise.

Godliness of Life

A Spirit-filled and a Spirit-led life is essential to soul winning (Ephesians 5:18; John 16:13-14; Zechariah 4:6). This spiritual fitness is conditioned by several things.

1. The Presentation of One's Body (Romans 6:13; 12:1-3)

This yielding of one's body is for a twofold purpose. First, it is for a *righteous* life, and then for a *useful* one. First to *be*, then to *do*. We must deliberately place all we are and have completely at His disposal, to *be* what

He wants us to be, and to *do* what He wants us to do, and to *go* where He wants us to go.

2. Dependence in Prayer

The work is God's; therefore we must speak much to Him about it. God inspires, hears, and answers believing prayer. Prayer is, at the same time, a confession of our own inadequacy, and a confidence in Divine ability to supply all the needs. We should pray for opportunities for personal work, guidance in it, and wisdom for it (James 1:5-6; Jeremiah 33:3; John 14:12-15; Matthew 17:21).

3. Purity of Life (Isaiah 52:11)

Cleanliness of life is essential to usefulness in service. We must have purity of thought (Philippians 4:8), purity of speech, truthfulness (Ephesians 4:25) and purity of deed, honesty (1 Peter 2:11-12; Philippians 2:12-16; 2 Peter 3:11; 1 Thessalonians 2:10; 2 Timothy 2:21).

4. Purpose of Heart

A holy determination to obey God's Word and His leading is vital. Clay Trumbull, who wrote the book entitled, *Taking Men Alive,* states his purpose of heart thus, "Whenever I was in such intimacy with a soul as to be justified in choosing my theme of conversation, the theme of themes should have prominence between us; so that I might learn his need and, if possible, meet it." He adhered to this determination for 50 years, and was greatly used of God in soul winning.

5. Meekness of Spirit

"The meek will He guide" (Psalm 25:9). Meekness is not weakness, but strength under perfect control. Christ is the perfect example of meekness (Matthew 11:28-30). We must realize our own insufficiency and rely entirely on His strength (2 Corinthians 3:5-6; 12:7-10; John 15:5). Thus we will be humble, but not servile; confident, but not self-opinionated.

Courage

There is a natural timidity about each one of us. After many years of soul winning, Trumbull confessed that he was still as timid when approaching a soul as he had been 50 years before. Some Christians find it easier than others (Jeremiah 1:8-10; Isaiah 12:2-3; Joshua 1:9; Psalm 34:4). Note "all my fears." God knows your personality and disposition, and His commands become His enablings. Real courage consists in going on, even when afraid. Remember, the person you approach is just as scared of you as you are of him, so cheer up! Are you afraid? Then read Psalm 27:1, 14; 56:3; Isaiah 12:2. Are you weak? Then read Isaiah 40:29-31; Ephesians 1:19; 6:10-11; Romans 14:4. Do not expect tomorrow's grace today. "As thy days, so shall thy strength be" (Deuteronomy 33:25).

Guidance

This includes tact in approach. Tact is not always a gift, but must be acquired by constant practice. Put yourself in the other person's place. How would you like to be approached?

Tact has been described as, "The art of putting ourselves in the place of others, so that we might know their needs, and supply them; realize their prejudices, and conciliate them. It is the intuitive perception of what is proper and fitting, and of saying and doing the right thing at the right time, so as not to unnecessarily offend, or anger." The meaning of the word "tact" is "touch." Thus we are to touch a soul in the right place, at the right time, and in the right way. The right combination of the ideal Christian worker is a cool head and a warm heart. To have a cold head and a cold heart results in a deadly, chilling formality. To have a hot head and a hot heart is to become fanatical and unbalanced.

A beautiful example of this tact is found in John 4. Study Christ's tact in dealing with this woman. Tact is doing exactly what is expedient or suitable in every circumstance (John 4:7). Tact is putting yourself in another's place in order to discover his needs and supply them; to persuade and to break down prejudice (John 4:9-10, 13-15). Tact is knowing how to deal with a man or woman in order, first to win him for yourself, and then to the Lord (John 4:9, 29). Tact is a work of the imagination. It lays its plans carefully so that the prospect cannot escape God's claim on him (John 4:16-19).

More Requirements

Pray for special guidance and wisdom as to whom to speak. We cannot, nor are we expected, to speak to all, but only to those whom the Lord would have us (Acts 8:29). This involves spiritual alertness and prompt obedience to God's guidance. Dr. Torrey used to pray that the Lord would cause those to whom he should speak to occupy the seat alongside him on a train journey. An old friend of mine in Scotland used to take it as from the Lord that all who approached him and asked him the time of the day were the ones to whom he should speak concerning salvation. Each evening he took a walk in a park, and never failed to have an opportunity through this simple plan.

Pray for guidance and wisdom as to what to say, and how to say it. How are you to approach and make contact with the individual? For such work, "We need wisdom beyond our own, to win the souls of men. . . . There is no work so effective, so romantic, so enduring, and so glorious" (S. Chadwick).

To sum up: Soul winning must be done in a spirit of prayerfulness, in absolute dependence on the Lord; with real humility of soul, with the meekness that characterized the Master, with genuine earnestness, and with a confident assurance in the Savior whom we represent and the gospel we proclaim.

Verses to Memorize

For God so loved the world, that he gave his only begotten Son, that whosoever believeth in him should not perish, but have everlasting life.	All that the Father giveth me shall come to me; and him that cometh to me I will in no wise cast out.
He that believeth on the Son hath everlasting life: and he that believeth not the Son shall not see life; but the wrath of God abideth on him.	If any man will do his will, he shall know of the doctrine, whether it be of God, or whether I speak of myself.
Verily, verily, I say unto you, He that heareth my word, and believeth on him that sent me, hath everlasting life, and shall not come into condemnation; but is passed from death unto life.	Then said Jesus again unto them, I go my way, and ye shall seek me, and shall die in your sins: whither I go, ye cannot come.
Marvel not at this: for the hour is coming, in the which all that are in the graves shall hear his voice, And shall come forth; they that have done good, unto the resurrection of life; and they that have done evil, unto the resurrection of damnation.	Jesus answered them, Verily, verily, I say unto you, Whosoever committeth sin is the servant of sin.

John 6:37	John 3:16
John 7:17	John 3:36
John 8:21	John 5:24
John 8:34	John 5:28-29

Chapter 5

Hindrances

Since soul winning, through personal evangelism, is so essential and so greatly blessed of God, why are more Christians not engaged in it? This chapter will attempt to answer this question by viewing *negatively* what we have stated *positively* in the previous section.

The Fear of Man (Proverbs 29:25)

Many Christians have allowed themselves to be silenced in their witness by their fear of the reproach and ridicule of men. The thought of being viewed as "peculiar" by the ungodly, or even by the carnal Christian, has robbed thousands of their courage to testify for Christ. What a tragedy this is!

God's path for His people has never been a popular one. This fact was plainly stated by the Son of God Himself (John 15:18-21; Matthew 5:11-12). It is evident from the book of Acts where the history of the early Church was one of constant persecution. The Epistles make clear that the "offence of the cross" has not ceased (Galatians 5:11). The cross is an offence to *morality*, because neither works nor character can fit a man for the presence of God (Galatians 2:16); to *philosophy*, because it appeals to faith and not to human reason, or secular learning (1 Corinthians 1:19-31); to *culture*, because its truth is revealed to babes (Matthew 11:25); to *caste*, because God chooses the poor and the humble (James 2:1-6); and to *the will*, because it calls for unconditional surrender (Romans 8:7-8).

We live in a world that despised, rejected, and crucified the Lord of glory. Its attitude to Him is still unchanged. Therefore the Christian must be prepared to face courageously the opposition bound to rise against him as he lifts up his voice for his Master and seeks to live to His glory. The adherents of false cults seem to have little or no timidity in propagating their erroneous doctrines. Salesmen seem to suffer from no inferiority complex as they go from house to house selling their wares and insurance agents suffer no embarrassment pointing out the advantages of taking out a life insurance policy. Surely, as "ambassadors for Christ," we should, at

His command, go forth boldly to witness for Him, and worthily represent the One who saved us by His grace (2 Corinthians 5:20; Acts 4:13). Torrey was once asked the best method of soul winning. He replied, "Go and do it!" Courage can be developed by practice.

Prayerlessness

The Lord Jesus has left us an example that we should "follow his steps." This applies to prayer, as in every other aspect of the Christian life (1 Peter 2:21). How often it is recorded of Him that He prayed, sometimes the whole night through. If He needed prayer, how much more we!

When the *Titanic* struck an iceberg and sank the *Californian* was close by, but her fires were banked and the radio engineer was fast asleep. The distress signals of the doomed vessel passed unheard. She was "out of touch," and the opportunity of a lifetime was lost forever. Prayer prepares the servant of the Lord both to know and do the will of his Master. To neglect prayer is to lose sensitiveness to the Spirit's leading (Isaiah 11:2-3). The Christian is altogether too busy for God who has no time for prayer. Make and take time to supplicate the throne of grace for only thus can you do effective service (Luke 18:1; 6:12; Matthew 9:37-38; James 5:17-18; 1 Samuel 12:23).

Secret Sin

Any harmful habit that defiles our conscience, beclouds our spiritual faculties, weakens our sensitiveness to the Spirit's leading, or robs us of communion with God and the joy of His service must be resolutely confessed and turned from as *sin* (Psalm 51:12-13). John closes his epistle with the words, "Little children, keep yourselves from idols." An idol is anything that displaces God in the affections. It may be something quite legitimate in itself, but if it robs Christ of the preeminence in the life, or obscures our spiritual vision, it must go (1 John 5:21). "Lay aside every weight" (Hebrews 12:1). Nothing can compensate for loss at the judgment seat of Christ (1 Corinthians 3:11-15; 9:27).

Ignorance of God's Word

Many say nothing because they have nothing to say; and they have nothing to say because they have not been listening to God. Children learn to talk by hearing and talking: so must we (Isaiah 50:4-5). We need "opened ears" if we are to have "opened lips" (Psalm 51:15).

Just as a doctor studies and "reads up" on his case, so we must apply ourselves to the Scriptures. We must learn what God has to say about the disease of the sinner and the remedy that God prescribes. "Where there is no vision, the people perish" (Proverbs 29:18). Are people perishing because of your ignorance (Hosea 4:6)? Often, during the course of evangelistic meetings, I have approached people who have been Christians for many years and asked them to speak to some anxious soul, only to hear them reply, "I'm sorry, but I don't have any experience in that sort of thing!" Just imagine! A Christian of mature years not knowing how to lead a soul to Christ! There are many such. Each Christian should earnestly seek after such knowledge (Proverbs 2:1-6; 3:13-18; Titus 1:9; 2 Timothy 2:15).

Selfishness

Soul winning is not easy work, for it calls for strenuous effort and self-denial. It costs time, money and energy. Many will give this effort to further their own business, but not for "the Father's business" (Luke 2:49). Many a so-called "successful business man" has "failed of the grace of God" (Hebrews 12:15).

Self preservation may be the first law of nature, but it is certainly not a law of grace (2 Corinthians 5:14-15; Luke 14:26-27; Romans 12:11). Carey, who opened India to the gospel, when asked, "What is your business?" replied, "My business is to preach the gospel, and I cobble shoes to pay expenses." Many a young Christian, who has evidenced no desire to go and preach the gospel at his Lord's command, has been compelled to respond when drafted by his country. Whether willingly, or reluctantly, he has had to exchange the comforts of civilization for the privations and horrors of war. There is surely no question as to which call was the more important. If one is prepared to sacrifice himself for one's country, why not for Christ?

Garibaldi, the liberator of Italy, addressed himself to those who volunteered their services in his cause, "I offer you hardship, hunger, rags, thirst, sleepless nights, footsores, privations innumerable, and victory in the noblest cause that ever asked you!" Men responded to that challenge. May we respond to Christ's, "Come, take up your cross, and follow me."

Callousness

Notice Christ's compassion for the lost. His was the compassion of a shepherd for lost sheep (Mark 6:34); of a physician for a patient (Matthew 14:14); of a benefactor for the hungry (Matthew 15:32); of a comforter for the bereaved (Luke 7:13); of a deliverer for the oppressed (Mark 5:19). It should be a cause for concern if we are not concerned for the lost. John Knox cried, "Give me Scotland, or I die!" Notice Paul's concern (Romans 9:1-3). See Jeremiah's cry (Jeremiah 9:1). Christ wept as He viewed doomed Jerusalem (Luke 19:41).

Our callousness will surely disappear if we face four facts in the presence of God. Think of *God's plain statements regarding the lost* (Romans 3:10-19; 6:23; 1 Corinthians 1:18). Remember *the love of God* as shown in the gift of His Son (1 John 4:9; John 3:16). Think of *the love of Christ* as demonstrated by the sacrifice of Himself for sinners (1 John 3:16). Ponder *the awful doom of the Christ rejecter* (Revelation 20:11-15; Mark 9:43-48; Matthew 25:30-46).

The story is told of a California gold digger who was returning by ship to his home. His hoard of precious gold dust was carried in a belt worn around his body. The ship took fire not far from land. Being a strong swimmer, he thought that even with the weight of the gold he could swim safely to land. As he prepared to leave the vessel, a little girl approached him and asked most piteously, "Won't you please save me?" Then the struggle began. He knew he could not save both the girl and his gold. One or the other must be left behind. Throwing away his belt of gold he took the little girl and swam with her to safety. Do we not hear voices coming from earth's Christless millions pleading, "Won't you please save me?" Let us cast away all that hinders in the way of selfish gain, pleasure and ease, and devote ourselves to the task!

> "O, for a passionate passion for souls!
>   O, for a pity that yearns!
> O, for a love that loves unto death!
>   O, for a fire that burns!
> O, for a prayer power that prevails,
>   That pours itself out for the lost!
> Victorious prayer in the Conqueror's name,
>   Whatever may be the cost!"

Verses to Memorize

He that is of God heareth God's words: ye therefore hear them not, because ye are not of God.	And when he is come, he will reprove the world of sin, and of righteousness, and of judgment: Of sin, because they believe not on me; Of righteousness, because I go to my Father, and ye see me no more; Of judgment, because the prince of this world is judged.
And I give unto them eternal life; and they shall never perish, neither shall any man pluck them out of my hand. My Father, which gave them me, is greater than all; and no man is able to pluck them out of my Father's hand.	But these are written, that ye might believe that Jesus is the Christ, the Son of God; and that believing ye might have life through his name.
Jesus said unto her, I am the resurrection, and the life: he that believeth in me, though he were dead, yet shall he live: And whosoever liveth and believeth in me shall never die. Believest thou this?	Neither is there salvation in any other: for there is none other name under heaven given among men, whereby we must be saved.
Jesus saith unto him, I am the way, the truth, and the life: no man cometh unto the Father, but by me.	Be it known unto you therefore, men and brethren, that through this man is preached unto you the forgiveness of sins: And by him all that believe are justified from all things, from which ye could not be justified by the law of Moses.

John 16:8-11	John 8:47
John 20:31	John 10:28-29
Acts 4:12	John 11:25-26
Acts 13:38-39	John 14:6

Chapter 6

Types of Sinner

The subjects of personal evangelism consist of every human being, but for the sake of convenience we shall group them into several distinct classes. We shall discuss the method of dealing with each of these classes later on.

The Careless

This person is by far the most common type and, perhaps, the most difficult. The average man seems absolutely indifferent to eternal realities. He is immersed in his business, his home life, or his pleasures. These are his horizons, and he does not wish to see any further. If thoughts of God, sin, death, and eternity penetrate his consciousness, as they will at times, he dismisses them from his mind as quickly as possible. He does not shake his fist in the face of God or deny the existence of God; but he orders his life as though no such Being as God exists, and deliberately shuts his eyes to such realities as sin, salvation, death, and eternity. His motto is, "Let us eat, drink and be merry." Truly, "God is not in all his thoughts" (Luke 12:19; Psalm 10:4).

The problem in such a case is to arouse and awaken him to a sense of his need and danger and exclaim, "What meanest thou, O sleeper? Arise and call upon thy God" (Jonah 1:6).

The Deceived

These also form a common class. They have given ear to false teaching, and their minds consequently have been perverted from the truth. Very often the error that blinds them seems to have a foundation in the Word of God, due to a wrestling of the Scriptures, or to a false interpretation of the words, or to a text divorced from the context of the Scripture in which it is found (2 Peter 3:16).

One of the marks of the "last days" is the multiplicity of false teachers and wrong doctrines (1 Timothy 4:1-3; 2 Timothy 3:1-7; 4:3-4; Matthew 7:15-16; Acts 20:29). It matters not how ridiculous, illogical or unscriptural a theory may be; there will always be those who will lend a ready ear to it, and become enthusiastic in propagating the error. Adherents of false cults are often more zealous in spreading their false doctrines than Christians in preaching the truth of God! Among the deceived could be mentioned Seventh Day Adventists, Russellites or Jehovah's Witnesses, Christian Scientists, Mormons, Unitarians, Universalists, Theosophists, Spiritists, etc.

The problem is to deliver them from their false ideas, by the wise use of the Word of God. This is not an easy task for error seems to exercise an hypnotic influence on its victims and rob them of the capacity for clear thinking and logical discussion.

The Objector

This type of person is full of objections, mostly of a second-hand variety, which he tries to convince himself are original, and which he imagines are unanswerable. He questions the authority of the Bible and announces that it is "full of contradictions." He objects to being classified as a lost and guilty sinner, and to being informed that he cannot save himself by any efforts of his own. He particularly objects to "hypocrites" and leaves the impression that all personal workers belong to that same category. He wants to know, if there is a God, why does He allow this or that, and points to all the injustice that prevails in the world. When cornered, he will even pretend to have an interest in foreign missions and inquire, "What about the heathen?"

The problem in this case is to meet his objections calmly, courteously, and faithfully from the Word of God. This is not so difficult, as most of his objections are of the stock variety. Often, of course, these objections are only a blind to give him an excuse for continuing in his sin.

The Agnostic, Skeptic, and Atheist

The Agnostic declares that no one can know whether God is, or is not; whether the Bible is the Word of God or not; whether salvation is real or only imaginary; or whether there is a heaven or a hell. The agnostic denies the possibility of knowing, with certainty and finality, the fundamental doctrines of the Christian faith.

The Skeptic frankly confesses his unbelief in the existence of God and in the whole Bible as the revelation from God. He is an unbeliever, and has no hesitation about expressing his contempt for Christianity and the God of Christianity.

The Atheist denies flatly that there is any God at all. He seeks to explain the phenomena of creation by natural causes.

The problem here is to show to each that God is, that He has revealed Himself fully and finally in His Word, and particularly in His Son, the Savior of all men.

The Excuser

He has plentiful supply of excuses by which he covers up his real reasons for not trusting Christ and becoming a Christian. Someone has said that an excuse is a statement of the circumstances surrounding our failure to do what we know we ought to have done. There is nothing new in excuses. They began in the Garden of Eden and have gone on ever since (Genesis 3:10, 12-13; Luke 14:18).

The problem, as in the case of the objector, is to meet each excuse with a scriptural and logical answer. This will show the unreasonableness of the excuse in the light of both the Word of God and common sense.

The Ignorant

These have never heard the gospel and have never read any literature concerning God, Christ, and salvation. This class is more numerous than we suspect, for there are many in our midst who are just as ignorant of Christianity as the unreached tribes of Africa.

The problem here is to enlighten them by proclaiming the fact of God and His revelation. The missionary is faced with a similar task as he penetrate to regions where the gospel has never been heard.

The Anxious

This person has been convicted of his sin and need of salvation but he is not yet saved. He would like to be, but he doesn't know how. There are many such, far more than we imagine. They are longing for someone to speak to them, and it is indeed a blessed day when the convicted and anxious sinner is brought into touch with an earnest and intelligent personal soul winner.

The problem here is to lead the anxious soul to an intelligent apprehension of the finished work of Christ, a reception of Him as Savior, and an acknowledgment of Him as Lord of the life.

The Confused

The person has been convinced of his need as a lost sinner. He has heard the gospel and, perhaps, has even been dealt with by an unintelligent worker. He is full of forebodings, fears and doubts. He is occupied largely with his own feelings, ideas and difficulties. He imagines he has "committed the unpardonable sin," or has "sinned away the day of grace," or he says, "I have tried before and failed." Like Bunyan's pilgrim, he flounders in the Bog of Despondency waiting for someone to help him out of his doubts, darkness and despair.

The problem, in this case, is to direct his thoughts with God's Word from himself to Christ, and from his feelings to the Scripture.

The Backslider

These were once joyous Christians but now are the most miserable of people. They have lost the joy and, in some cases, the assurance of their salvation. Like Naomi they have to say, "Call me not Naomi (pleasant) but Mara (bitter)" (Ruth 1:20). Their harps have been hung in the willows and they have no songs to sing (Psalm 137:1-4, compare 126:1-4).

The problem with this person is to seek to bring about a restoration of soul. This can only come through the confession and forsaking of his sin. This will result in soul revival so that once again he will be enabled to "joy in the God of his salvation."

The Discouraged Christian

This discouragement may be due to adversity in business, loss of health, bereavement in the family, or the trials of life. While in this condition they are neither inclined, nor fit to be of much help to anyone.

The problem is to discover the cause and seek to "strengthen their hand in God" (1 Samuel 23:16). See also 2 Corinthians 1:3-4; 1 Thessalonians 5:14. By doing so we shall become "fellow helpers to the truth" (3 John 8).

Verses to Memorize

And the times of this ignorance God winked at; but now commandeth all men everywhere to repent.	But to him that worketh not, but believeth on him that justifieth the ungodly, his faith is counted for righteousness.
For I am not ashamed of the gospel of Christ: for it is the power of God unto salvation to every on that believeth; to the Jew first, and also to the Greek.	For when we were yet without strength, in due time Christ died for the ungodly.
Now we know that what things so ever the law saith, it saith to them who are under the law; that every mouth may be stopped, and all the world may become guilty before God.	For the wages of sin is death; but the gift of God is eternal life through Jesus Christ our Lord.
For all have sinned, and come short of the glory of God.	For I know that in me (that is, in my flesh,) dwelleth no good thing: for to will is present with me; but how to perform that which is good I find not.

Romans 4:5	Acts 17:30
Romans 5:6	Romans 1:16
Romans 6:23	Romans 3:19
Romans 7:18	Romans 3:23

Chapter 7

Methods in General

In soul winning, it is a case of "many men, many minds and many methods." No hard and fast rules can be laid down. We can only state some *general principles* for the methods will vary with the subject and God's particular leading.

No two human beings are exactly alike for each person possesses a personality which distinguishes him from every other individual on the face of the earth. Personality is a difficult thing to define. It consists of the impression we make on others because of what we *are*, intellectually, emotionally, and volitionally. I am what I am because of what I know, feel, and do. This, in turn, is conveyed to others as we come in touch with them. The task of the soul winner is to study the best means to reach the intellect, stir the emotions, and bring the will to the point of surrender to Christ. Only God is "sufficient for these things" (2 Corinthians 3:5-6).

However, some characteristics are common to the human race as a whole. "As in water face answereth to face, so the heart of man to man" (Proverbs 27:19). In other words we see ourselves reflected in our fellow men. Our reactions are largely theirs. Would we wish to be approached in a kindly and courteous manner? Well, so would they. Would we resent rudeness, arrogance, and condescension? So also will they.

A study of the different types of inquirer seen in the New Testament is helpful in determining the best methods to employ. Saul of Tarsus was a determined, bigoted, self-righteous man. The appeal was made to his *will;* hence he says, "What *wilt* Thou have me to do?" (Acts 9). The eunuch was approached by way of his *intellect* for Philip inquired, "*Understandest* thou what thou readest?" (Acts 8:30). In the case of Lydia it was the *emotions,* or the affections, that had the emphasis, for we read, "Whose *heart* the Lord opened." What would not have touched Saul, or the eunuch, stirred her to the depths. With the jailer at Philippi it was the *conscience* that was aroused and a sense of sin and fear produced; hence the earthquake was sent. Imagine the effect if the earthquake method had been applied to Lydia! She would have died of shock!

Naturalness in our methods is the best thing. In this, as in everything else, be yourself. There is always the danger of imitating others and becoming artificial. It is good to observe others as they do personal work and also to listen to all the advice that experienced Christian workers can give us; but in the actual *doing* of it be yourself. David is a good example in his refusal to wear the armor of Saul (1 Samuel 17:38-39). Adopt what suggestions appeal to you, but remember, you will learn mostly by your mistakes anyway!

Things to Do

1. Diagnose the Case

This can only be done as he unburdens his heart to you willingly; or as you draw him out by tactful questioning. In this way you can discover to which class he belongs. This is like a doctor's examination. He lets the patient describe his symptoms and supplements the description by judicious questions to clarify the case to him. How different is this from the quack medicine vender who has but one remedy for all ills—his own particular medicine! Some good questions to ask would be, "What do you think it means to become a Christian?" "Why do you wish to become a Christian?" "How do you think you can become a Christian?" A person's answers to these questions will inform you where he stands and how best to deal with him.

2. Describe the Disease

Here is the greatest need for thoroughness and faithfulness. We must leave the person we are helping in no doubt. Using skillfully God's Word, we must probe deep and expose the cancer of sin. We must beware of being a "peace, peace" worker (Jeremiah 8:11). Show the person his need as one born in sin, having a deceitful heart, guilty of sinful thoughts, words and deeds, lost and helpless to save himself, and doomed if he dies in that condition. All pride, smugness, and self-sufficiency must be brought to an end, and only God's Word can do it. The *right* Scripture must be applied to the *right* person, in the *right* way at the *right* time. This calls for the Spirit's guidance and makes us dependent on God. "Salvation is of the Lord" (Jonah 2:9). We must learn to make haste *slowly*.

3. Prescribe the Remedy

Be very plain, and make *each step* clear from the Word of God. Find out, by questioning, whether or not the person sees from the Scriptures the truth you are seeking to impress upon his mind. Do not put words into his mouth. Let him describe in his own words what he understands from the Scripture he has read, and you can then judge whether or not he has grasped its import. It is "the entrance of the word that gives light" (Psalm 119:130). Make much of the Word of God and the Christ of God, for the one reveals the Other.

Once the person realizes his lost condition show him the love of God for sinners and the proof of that love in the gift of His Son. Exalt the redemptive work of Christ on the cross and point out its all-sufficiency to meet his need. Explain simply the way of salvation and what is involved in believing the Word, receiving the Savior, and confessing Christ as Lord of his life (Romans 10:9-10).

4. Warn of Danger

Do this faithfully, for "faithful are the wounds of a friend." Point out to the person the peril of dying in his sins (John 8:21); of hardening his heart to the Word of God (Hebrews 3:12-15; Proverbs 29:1); of resisting the Spirit's strivings (Acts 7:51); of procrastination (Hebrew 2:3; Proverbs 27:1), and of Christ's second coming (Matthew 25:1-13; Luke 13:24-25).

5. Urge an Immediate Decision

Do not *force* it. You cannot decide for him; this is entirely up to him. Beware of high pressure evangelism, or of salvation by formula. By this we mean the answer in the affirmative, to a series of questions put to him. Here is a sample of this formula: "You are a sinner, aren't you?" "Yes." "Do you believe Jesus died for sinners?" "Yes." "Therefore He must have died for you, didn't He?" "Yes." "You will trust Him as your Savior, won't you?" "Yes." "Well you are now saved!" Thus all this person had to do was to answer "Yes" four times to be saved! Slavish dependence on a formula such as the popular "Four Spiritual Laws" can also quickly become artificial.

After having made clear the gospel, ask, "What do you propose to do about this, seeing you profess to have seen your need as a lost sinner, and God's provision of salvation?" Let the person answer in his own words. If he declares his intention of trusting Christ, get him to pray out loud and, in his own words, to tell the Lord Jesus that he now receives Him as his own Savior.

6. Anchor Him to the Word for His Assurance

Point out such Scriptures as John 3:16; 5:24; 10:9; 1 John 5:13.

7. Get Him to Confess Christ

Confession of his faith in Christ is vital (Romans 10:9-10; Psalm 27:1; 2 Timothy 1:12; Mark 5:19). Also teach him to read the Scriptures, pray, live for Christ and serve Him (1 Peter 2:2; Psalm 119:9-10; Daniel 6:10; Isaiah 40:31; Mark 16:15).

Things to Avoid

The following suggestions are chiefly to help you in dealing with souls after a gospel meeting.

1. Don't Advertise Yourself

Keep Christ prominent, for Christianity is Christ (John 3:30). Don't give him a tract to read at this point for it will distract him. Good tracts can be given once the interview is over to reinforce what has been said and done.

2. Don't Deal with More Than One at a Time

Get him alone. Two is company, three's a crowd. A soul closes up like an oyster when the third party comes along. Let the other talk with God while you talk with the inquirer (Mark 8:22-26).

3. Don't Either Be Untidy or Overdressed

Be well groomed and be sure you use a mild mouthwash and a deodorant. Neither be gloomy, nor frivolous, for first impressions are important. Be yourself, humble, cheerful, and earnest.

4. Don't Monopolize the Conversation

If your prospect has a lot to say, let him say it. He will ultimately talk himself out and then you will have your opportunity.

5. Don't Deal with Those of the Opposite Sex

As a general rule, particularly if young, men should deal with men, and women with women. There are times when this cannot be done as when the inquirer asks particularly for you.

6. Don't Choose One Who Is Too Much Your Senior

Older people resent being instructed by one much younger than themselves.

7. Don't Be Drawn into an Argument

You may win the argument and lose the prospect. The Devil will seek to sidetrack you on this issue. Sometimes the inquirer will do it for a smoke screen under cover of which he can retire with haste.

8. Don't Tell the Inquirer Your Own Experience

Let him lean on the Word of God and he will have an experience all his own. Your testimony should not intrude.

9. Don't Multiply Texts and Illustrations

Far better to use two or three, and hammer them home, than a dozen lightly touched on. These texts should not be *quoted*, but shown to the *seeker from the Bible,* so that he can read them for himself. God's Word will thus be honored and given the place of supreme authority (1 Corinthians 2:5). Let the inquirer rest on a "thus saith the Lord." For instance, supposing you are showing the inquirer John 3:1-5, after he has read these verses you could ask him, "What does Christ say is essential to seeing the kingdom of God?" "To whom did He say this?" "Who needs to be born again?" He cannot answer, "Yes," or "No," to any of these questions. They can only be answered by him as he again refers to the Word of God.

10. Don't Be Unduly Familiar

Avoid putting your hand on his shoulder or around him, for he may resent it.

11. Don't Be in a Hurry

Make sure the seeker knows just what God's Word says. Question him about what he has read (Isaiah 28:16; Acts 8:30). Wesley once said, "I haven't time to be in a hurry." .

12. Don't Lose Your Temper

Even if you have cause to be ruffled, keep control of yourself. Read 2 Timothy 2:24-25.

13. Don't Say, "You Have Only to Believe to Be Saved"

This is dangerous unless he knows what and whom to believe.

14. Don't Minimize What Is Involved

Becoming a Christian involves accepting Christ as Savior and owning Him as Lord. It means "good-bye" to the self life. Make this clear.

15. Don't Interrupt Another Christian Worker

If he calls on you for assistance, well and good. Don't let anyone interrupt you. In case you are not able to deal properly with your inquirer, it may be well to pass him on to a more experienced worker.

16. Don't Tell a Person He Is Saved

God can do this much better than you and it will be far more convincing. If they ask, "Am I saved?" turn them back to the Word of God and reply, "What does God say?"

17. Don't Be Discouraged by Apparent Failure

Often you are simply another link in the chain of grace that brings a sinner to Christ. Someone has said, "God never gives a man a whole soul." Impressions have been formed by others before us, and shall be made after us. We often "enter into the labor of others" (John 4:37-38). Let us keep at the job, for "in due season we shall reap if we faint not" (Galatians 6:9).

18. Don't Give the Impression That "No!" Is a Final Answer

Always try to leave a person with the impression that the conversation may be reopened whenever you desire.

19. Don't Be Afraid to Say "I Don't Know"

Some questions you will be asked have puzzled the wisest philosophers. Bring him back to the main issue.

20. Don't Withhold Praise

Commend what is good in the inquirer's answers, or in his statements to you. Give him credit for what he does know, and lead him from that to a knowledge of what he doesn't know.

Verses to Memorize

And not only they, but ourselves also, which have the firstfruits of the Spirit, even we ourselves groan within ourselves, waiting for the adoption, with the redemption of our body	But the natural man receiveth not the things of the Spirit of God: for they are foolishness unto him: neither can he to know them, because they are spiritually. discerned.
That if thou shalt confess with thy mouth the Lord Jesus, and shalt believe in thine heart that God hath raised him from the dead, thou shalt be saved.	For I delivered unto you first of all that which I also received, how that Christ died for our sins according to the scriptures; And that he was buried, and that he rose again the third day according to the scriptures.
For whosoever shall call upon the name of the Lord shall be saved.	But if our gospel be hid, it is hid to them that are lost: In whom the god of this world hath blinded the minds of them which believe not, lest the light of the glorious gospel of Christ, who is the image of God, should shine unto them.
For the preaching of the cross is to them that perish foolishness; but unto us which are saved it is the power of God.	Therefore if any man be in Christ, he is a new creature: old things are passed away; behold, all things are become new.

1 Corinthians 2:14	Romans 8:23
1 Corinthians 15:3-4	Romans 10:9
2 Corinthians 4:3-4	Romans 10:3
2 Corinthians 5:17	1 Corinthians 1:18

Chapter 8

The Right Approach

Types of Approach

The problem of how rightly to approach a person is a very real one, and one that may well keep you on your knees. Earnestly pray for wisdom and seek to develop the gift of approach. Pray for openings for personal conversation and take them when they present themselves. Thus you can often answer your own prayers. You might make many mistakes but you can profit by the experience.

1. The Direct Approach

This could be termed "shock tactics." It is the abrupt introduction of the vital theme. Many use this method to very good advantage. This is sometimes necessary because of the shortness of time.

John Vassar, a great soul winner, was a past master in this art. He wasted no time in preliminaries but cleared the deck for immediate action. He would ask a perfect stranger, "Is your soul right with God?" "Do you know your sins are forgiven?" "Are you saved?" "Are you ready to meet God?" "Where will you be in eternity?" One of his best friends said he did not know of a single instance when John was rebuffed for his audacity. He believed that this was the method that God would have him adopt and was mightily used of God.

My own brother was approached in London, England, by a well dressed gentleman who inquired courteously, "Pardon me, may I ask you a question?" When he had received permission, he asked, "Is your soul right with God?" He then went on to inform my brother that he had promised God he would ask this question once each day of an individual.

Another friend of mine never inquired of a person whether he was saved or a Christian. He argued that if the person answered, "Yes," when he should have said "No," he could not go any further with him in the matter, except at the risk of calling him untruthful. Instead, he would say, "Isn't it a grand thing to know that one's sins are all forgiven?" or, "My, what a wonderful thing it is to be born again!" or, "It certainly is good to be saved!" He would then watch the reaction on the part of this person. If he brightened up and replied, "Yes, praise God," then he would know he was a Christian. If, however, he hesitated or mumbled something about "hoping so," my friend would start right in dealing with him about his soul. It can be readily seen that there is real merit in all these ways of direct approach.

2. The Indirect Approach

The first method does not commend itself to all. Some prefer the indirect method and have become expert in the art of turning a conversation which began with the weather, or some other secular subject, into spiritual channels. This requires real skill, but skill can be developed with practice. Whatever the subject of a conversation may be at the start, it can be deftly directed to the theme of themes, so that the person actually imagines he has introduced the subject himself!

3. The Interrogation Approach

By this is meant using skillful questions to arouse the interest and lead the person to reveal his own spiritual needs. I had a friend who was an expert at this type of approach. He would ask, "Excuse me, but could you tell me how a sinner can get right with a holy God?" When the person murmured something about "doing the best he could," he would take out his Bible and turn to Ephesians 2:8-9 and say, "That's what I used to think once, but this verse says, 'Not of works, lest any man should boast.'" From this point on he would tell just how a sinner could be saved. This man was greatly used of God.

4. The Good Deed Approach

Putting the person under an obligation to you can often open doors. Do a person a favor and a splendid opportunity is provided for spiritual contact. A Christian friend of mine heard of a sick woman. She went into the home, made her a cup of coffee, did the dishes, washed the children, and tidied the house. Then she read to her from the Scriptures and spoke of Christ. The whole family was won. Her favor had disarmed all opposition.

The Right Approach

Many opportunities of speaking to people about Christ await the person who is really looking for them, and is willing to pay the price, in the way of hard work and self-denial. Many a mother, whose children prevent her from going to a gospel meeting, might be persuaded to go if someone would look after her children while she went to hear the gospel. Many a mother has been won for the Savior by this means.

5. The "Can You Help Me, Please" Approach

Put oneself under an obligation to a person. Most people appreciate being asked to do a little favor. Christ Himself adopted this method in dealing with the woman at the well. When the favor has been shown, and you have thanked him, you can repay the debt by doing him a favor, and telling him of the One who did you the greatest of all favors by saving your soul.

6. The Literature Approach

This is probably the easiest way of approaching a person. The tract should be given in a kindly and courteous manner. This will break the ice and open up the way of a personal conversation. I know a man who *lends* gospel tracts and books. When he calls again to have his tract or book returned, he finds out by questioning what the reaction to it has been. He could easily have given the tract but he prefers this method as it leaves the way open for further conversation. It is a good plan always to carry a few good gospel tracts with you which you have read yourself. You can thus better suit the booklet to the individual need of the person approached. Tracts should be appropriate, well written, attractively printed, easy to read, and clean. Dog-eared, grubby tracts should not be given out.

7. The After Meeting Approach

Be prayerful and on the lookout for strangers attending meetings. Approach such with a warm welcome. The comment, "That was a fine gospel message!" may provoke a favorable reply and an opening for conversation. Care should be taken not to force the conversation. If the person is not interested, invite him back again and tell him how glad you are to have him attend. Many a stranger to a gospel meeting has been scared away permanently by an overzealous "buttonholer" who insisted on forcing the issue. Here is where tact comes in.

Two Scriptural Examples

1. Our Savior Himself

Read John 4 and note how the Lord dealt with the woman at the well. He went out of His way to meet her (verse 4). He was not bound by conventionality (verse 9). He acted circumspectly; He chose high noon (verse 6, compare 1 Thessalonians 5:22). He put Himself to inconvenience to meet her (verse 6). He was tactful. He waited till they were alone (verse 8); He did not reproach or scold; He asked a favor (verse 7); He sought to teach a spiritual truth from a homely metaphor (verse 10); He began to get at close quarters (verse 16); He refused to be diverted when she raised the question of religion (verses 19-20); He did not ignore the points she raised as to the barriers of sex (verse 9), race (verse 9), and religion (verse 20). He revealed her sin and need (verse 18). He revealed Himself as Messiah (verse 26). Here is the great objective of all personal work, to lead the soul to a knowledge of Christ.

2. Philip the Evangelist

Read Acts 8:26-40 and see how Philip dealt with the Ethiopian. First he went near (verse 29). He wasn't standoffish, or a snob. He didn't stand on his dignity, or think it beneath him to talk to one soul. He was swift to do God's will. He ran. He didn't dawdle or waste time. His was a holy earnestness to grasp the opportunity while it was his. He questioned the Ethiopian. He didn't begin to give a formal message. He found out what the Ethiopian knew, and where he stood spiritually by judicious questioning. He sat with him. He put himself in his place. Here is tact at its best. He used the Scriptures to preach to him Jesus. He let the Word of God be seen, read, and applied. He led him to Christ. The moment came when the eunuch saw and bowed to the truth, believed on Christ, and owned Him as Lord. He got out of the way (verse 39). Philip left the convert with the Word of God in his hand, the Spirit in his heart, Christ as his Savior, and the joy of salvation in his soul.

Verses to Memorize

For he hath made him to be sin for us, who knew no sin; that we might be made the righteousness of God in him.	Christ hath redeemed us from the curse of the law, being made a curse for us: for it is written, Cursed is every one that hangeth on a tree.
And he said unto me, My grace is sufficient for thee: for my strength is made perfect in weakness. Most gladly therefore will I rather glory in my infirmities, that the power of Christ may rest upon me.	Be not deceived; God is not mocked: for whatsoever a man soweth, that shall he also reap.
Knowing that a man is not justified by the works of the law, but by the faith of Jesus Christ, even we have believed in Jesus Christ, that we might be justified by the faith of Christ, and not by the works of the law: for by the works of the law shall no flesh be justified.	In whom we have redemption through his blood, the forgiveness of sins, according to the riches of his grace.
For as many as are of the works of the law are under the curse: for it is written, Cursed is every one that continueth not in all things which are written in the book of the law to do them.	For by grace are ye saved through faith; and that not of yourselves: it is the gift of God: Not of works, lest any man should boast.

Galatians 3:13	2 Corinthians 5:21
Galatians 6:7	2 Corinthians 12:9
Ephesians 1:7	Galatians 2:16
Ephesians 2:8-9	Galatians 3:10

Chapter 9

The Careless and the Deceived

Again we emphasize there are no set rules we can follow in personal work, for no two souls are exactly alike. However, we can make suggestions that may be found useful. The human equation is always problematical. The best way to learn is by experience. *Do* it, and you will *know* how to do it. Practice makes perfect. The expert becomes such by constant practice. Some cases require special treatment (Matthew 17:21). We shall now consider how to deal with the subjects of personal evangelism as described in chapter six.

The Careless

Sometimes carelessness is only a mask to hide real, deep concern. A cynical smile is often used to conceal an aching heart due to soul distress. The work to be done with this class is sevenfold:

1. Awaken to a Sense of Need

This is not done by argument or persuasion, but by presenting appropriate Scriptures relying on the Spirit's work to produce conviction of sin. We cannot awaken this concern. Only God can do it and He does it principally through His Word. Therefore, the need to use it aright.

Point out the universality of sin (Romans 3:10-19, 23). Ask the person what is meant in this passage by, "There is none righteous," and "no, not one"; or what is meant by, "There is no difference"; or who is included in the word "all." Show that God's standard is absolute perfection and that His righteous requirements are found in the law (Luke 10:25-28). Ask him if he has kept this law perfectly. Dr. Torrey once showed a self righteous individual that he had committed the greatest sin by breaking the greatest commandment (Matthew 22:36-40). Use Isaiah 53:6; Mark 7:21-23; John 8:24; 3:36. All these Scriptures will not be used. Select what you consider the most appropriate to the occasion.

Point out the certainty of death and the judgment to follow (Hebrews 9:27; Romans 1:18; 6:23; 8:7-8; Acts 17:31; John 3:36; Revelation 20:11-15). Be faithful as well as kind. A surgeon used to say to his patients on whom he was to operate, "Take a good look at the wound, and then look at me until I get through." Let the inquirer get a good look at his sin, and then fix his eyes on Christ. He certainly should want to after that!

Point out the danger of rejecting or neglecting salvation (Hebrews 2:3; 10:28-29; John 3:17-18, 36; Proverbs 27:1; 29:1).

2. Point to Christ

When you are satisfied that real concern is manifested, make much of Christ's substitutionary sacrifice and show God's righteousness in the salvation of the sinner (1 Peter 2:24; 2 Corinthians 5:21; Isaiah 53:5-6; John 3:16; Romans 3:24-26).

3. Explain What It Means to Believe

God uses many words to convey what is involved by the word "believe." He uses the word:

a. *Look* (Isaiah 45:22). A child looks, with perfect confidence, to its parents for the provision of all its needs. A man looks to a friend who has promised to pay his debt. The idea is not to visualize Calvary, or conjure up the scene as a vision, but to confide in Christ and His work.

b. *Seek* (Isaiah 55:6). This necessitates an act of the will that evidences a genuine desire to know God.

c. *Call* (Romans 10:13). A child cries to its parents. A drowning man calls for rescue. Why does he cry? Because he is helpless to save himself and must rely upon another to save him.

d. *Come* (Matthew 11:28-30; Hebrews 7:25; Luke 14:17). This depicts the movement of the heart to Christ. Again, the act of the will is indicated. A child comes to the opened arms of its mother because it is invited. It is, therefore, the response of its will.

e. *Taste.* This means to partake, or to appropriate for oneself (Psalm 34:8). Food is of no value unless it is tasted and eaten.

f. *Take* (Revelation 22:17). Illustrate this aspect of believing by a wedding. "Wilt thou take this woman . . . this man?" The "I do" of both parties unites them in marriage. Both he and she consent, with the will, to take each other. Point out that Christ is willing to "take" him, and ask, "Will *you* 'take' Him?"

g. *Acquaint* (Job 22:21). This means to know. We get to know people by being introduced to each other. Seek to introduce the inquirer to Christ.

h. *Receive* (John 1:12). An armless man can receive a gift. How? By thanking you for it. He has received the gift in his heart though he cannot touch it with his hands.

i. *Submit* (James 4:7). This implies the surrender of one person to the authority of another. Christ demands unconditional surrender on the part of the sinner.

j. *Commit* (2 Timothy 1:12; Psalm 37:5). A patient commits himself to his doctor for an operation. He hands himself over unreservedly to his care.

k. *Believe* (Acts 16:30-31). To believe is to accept, as true, the word, the person, or the work of another. Remember, it is the *Object* of belief (Christ) and not the *belief* that saves. Occupation with *believing*, and not with *Christ*, has stumbled many. The emphasis is not on "believe," but on "the Lord Jesus Christ." The classic illustration is that of Blondin, the famous tight rope walker, who successfully pushed a man across the Niagara Falls in a wheelbarrow. He approached a boy and asked, "Do you believe I could wheel you across on that wire?" "Yes," replied the boy promptly. "All right, get in the barrow, and I'll wheel you across," said Blondin, but the boy refused, thus proving he really didn't believe, but merely gave mental assent to the possibility.

l. *Trust* (Isaiah 12:2). This is a lovely word and full of meaning. A man trusts his money to a bank, trusts his weight to a chair; a child trustingly jumps into the arms of its father.

4. Explain the Lordship of Christ

It means that from henceforth He is in absolute control of the life (Romans 10:9-10; 2 Corinthians 5:15). Christ is to be the Master of all he is and has.

5. Ask for a Definite Acceptance of Christ as Savior and Lord

Make sure he has really seen his need and grasped the way of salvation. Ask him, "Since you say you realize you are a lost and guilty sinner, and that Christ has done all the work needed for your salvation, what do you think you should do about it?" If he replies, "I should take Him as my Savior," then suggest that he get down on his knees and tell Christ that, in audible tones, with you as a witness to this solemn transaction. When he has done this, then join with him and give thanks to God for this soul that has trusted the Savior.

6. Show Him How to Be Sure He Is Saved

Point out that it is not his feelings, but God's Word that must be the foundation of his certainty (John 1:12; 5:24; 6:47; 10:9; 1 John 5:13; Romans 10:9-10). Mark some of these Scriptures on a piece of paper, so that he can refer to them again. Urge him to read a portion of the Word of God each day and start him on John's Gospel. Also press home upon him the need for prayer and praise.

7. Urge Him to Confess Christ

By telling others he nails his colors to the mast, or, to change the figure, burns his bridges behind him. Urge him henceforth to live for Christ alone and serve Him loyally. Consider using *a decision card*. This is useful, providing it is done *after a person has trusted Christ* for himself. The danger, otherwise, is that he imagines the signing of the card is the equivalent of trusting the Savior. It is the receiving of a Person, and not the signing of a card that saves. If he desires to have a decision card and sign it and keep it, see to it that the wording of the card is scriptural and leaves no doubt about what is involved by the signing of it.

He may not see all these seven things at one interview. I have known people to walk into a gospel meeting utterly indifferent to eternal things and, within an hour, be convicted of sin and soundly saved. I have known others who came to a hundred gospel meetings before they were finally reached and won for Christ. The Spirit's dealings are indeed mysterious and we cannot rush ahead of Him as He applies the Word of God to the sinner. Make certain the inquirer has grasped the *first* lesson before you attempt to teach him the second; for each lesson is based on the previous one and follows in logical succession.

The Deceived

These are many thousands of people who are deceived but imagine they are right. They are encouraged in their error by their false teachers and also by cleverly written tracts and books. In fact, in many cases, these deceived persons are more willing to do personal work with the Christian, than he with them! Before mentioning any of these false cults, it may be well to state a few general principles to keep in mind when dealing with them.

1. Be Acquainted with His Particular Belief

An excellent book for this purpose is *Heresies Exposed* by W. C. Irvine. A modern day classic is *Kingdom of the Cults* by Walter Martin. By studying such books you can discover exactly what their false doctrines are, and what Scriptures they wrongly use to back them up in their erroneous claims. Unless this is done, you will be working in the dark. To be forewarned is to be forearmed.

2. Remember He Sincerely Imagines That He Is Right

Often he is eager for the fray and quite prepared to carry the war to the enemy and try to convert the personal worker!

3. Do Not Unnecessarily Excite His Prejudices

Nothing is gained by needlessly antagonizing him. Here is where tact is required in full measure.

4. Do Not Be Drawn into Argument

There is a temptation to pit your knowledge and skill against his. This generates heat which, in turn, prevents the object you set about to accomplish (Ephesians 6:17; Hebrews 4:12-13). It is possible to win the argument and lose your prospect.

5. Be Courteous

Let any rudeness that may arise be shown on the other side (1 Corinthians 13:4-5; 2 Timothy 2:24-26).

6. Be Sympathetic

Put yourself in his place. Consider his environment. He may have been brought up in an atmosphere of false doctrine. Error, as we have before noted, exercises an hypnotic spell over its victims.

7. Be Patient

Do not get either discouraged or disgusted. Plow deep and take plenty of time to be thorough.

8. Avoid Side Issues

Keep to the main issue and do not allow yourself to be sidetracked by a discussion of the merits of one particular system of religion against another. Avoid personalities, but keep the Person of Christ ever before him.

Verses to Memorize

Finally, brethren, whatsoever things are true, whatsoever things are honest, whatsoever things are just, whatsoever things are pure, whatsoever things are lovely, whatsoever things are of good report; if there be any virtue, and if there be any praise, think on these things.	This is a faithful saying, and worthy of all acceptation, that Christ Jesus came into the world to save sinners; of whom I am chief.
In whom we have redemption through his blood, even the forgiveness of sins.	All scripture is given by inspiration of God, and is profitable for doctrine, for reproof, for correction, for instruction in righteousness.
Let the word of Christ dwell in you richly in all wisdom; teaching and admonishing one another in psalms and hymns and spiritual songs, singing with grace in your hearts to the Lord.	They profess that they know God; but in works they deny him, being abominable, and disobedient, and unto every good work reprobate.
For this cause also thank we God without ceasing, because, when ye received the word of God which ye heard of us, ye received it not as the word of men, but as it is in truth, the word of God, which effectually worketh also in you that believe.	But unto the Son he saith, Thy throne, O God, is forever and ever: a scepter of righteousness is the scepter of thy kingdom.

1 Timothy 1:15	Philippians 4:8
2 Timothy 3:16	Colossians 1:4
Titus 1:16	Colossians 3:16
Hebrews 1:8	1 Thessalonians 2:13

Chapter 10

Dealing with Delusion and "Churchianity"

Jehovah's Witnesses

This cult denies the Deity of Christ and asserts He was but a created being. It denies the value of His atonement; the reality of His physical resurrection; the eternity of retribution upon those who die rejecting Christ. They teach there is a future probation for those who die unsaved. Many books have been written to show this error in its true light, and the student would do well to secure one. When dealing with such show the following.

1. The Essential and Eternal Deity of Christ

Study Isaiah 9:6; Micah 5:2; Matthew 1:23; John 1:1-3; Colossians 1:13-18; Romans 9:5; 1 Timothy 3:16; Hebrews 1:7-10.

2. The Eternal Value of His Substitutionary Sacrifice

Study Hebrews 9:26; 1 Peter 2:24; Isaiah 53:5-6.

3. The Literal Bodily Resurrection of Christ

Study John 2:19-22; Luke 24:39

4. The Eternal Character of the Christ Rejecter's Retribution

Study Luke 16:19-31; John 5:28-29; Revelation 20:11-15; 22:11; Matthew 25:46; 2 Thessalonians 1:9. "Destruction" does not mean annihilation (Hosea 13:9). The same word, "eternal," that is used to denote God's existence, also describes the duration of punishment.

The Seventh Day Adventists

This group is unsound on the substitutionary sacrifice of Christ; on His sinless humanity; on the relation of the believer to the law of Moses; and on the intermediate state of the dead, teaching what is called "soul sleep" (the false notion that a person who dies is unconscious after death until the resurrection of his body). Its adherents are subtle, and will try to capitalize on the seeming soundness of many of their views.

As in the case of the Jehovah's Witnesses, the need is to be well acquainted with the false theories and the favorite Scriptures which Seventh Day Adventists twist to suit their own viewpoint. The best and fullest argument against them is by an A. M. Canright, who was once one of their most prominent teachers. His Book *Seventh Day Adventism Renounced* is unanswerable.

The main points to emphasize should be studied.

1. The Believer Is Dead to the Law

The death of Christ on his behalf takes care of that (Romans 7:1-4; 10:3-9).

2. The Dispensation of the Law Is Done Away

Christ has ended that dispensation (2 Corinthians 3:6-11).

3. The Believer Is No Longer Under the Law

As a rule of life it is grace not law that governs the Christian (Galatians 2:16–3:13). The epistle to the Galatians strikes the death blow to Seventh Day Adventism.

4. The Sabbath Was a Sign Between Israel and God

Study Exodus 31:13-17. Observance of "days" is not Christian (Colossians 2:16). Every command of the Decalogue is reaffirmed in the New Testament *except* the fourth!

5. Soul Sleep Is Unscriptural

Refer them to 2 Corinthians 5:1-8 and Philippians 1:20-23. They quote from Ecclesiastes but this book views all from a natural standpoint. Its viewpoint is man "under the sun" (Ecclesiastes 9:5-10). The text refers only to the body but not to the soul. That the spirit does not "sleep" with the body is clear from 1 Corinthians 5:5; Luke 23:43-46; Acts 7:59; Matthew 10:28.

The Christian Scientist

This cult, which is neither Christian nor scientific, has a great hold upon thousands of people, including many in affluent circumstances. It denies nearly all the fundamentals of Christianity and, by denying the reality of matter, is quite evidently unscientific. It is the "philosophy of nothingness." It has four basic propositions—God is all in all; God is good, good is mind; everything is Spirit, nothing is matter; Life, God, omnipotent, good; deny death, evil, sin, disease. Disease, sin, evil, death; deny good, omnipotent, God, life (*Science and Health*, 1903 edition, page 113).

It is difficult to deal with such people. They affirm that God, Christ, and the Holy Spirit are mere principles and not Persons. They teach that sin is an unreality, that the Devil is non-existent, and that sickness and death are merely errors of mortal mind.

They do believe in the Scriptures as inspired but claim the same for Mary Baker Eddy's *Science and Health*. Seek to show from the Scriptures exactly what you would show the careless or indifferent.

The Spiritist

Spiritism denies the personality of God, the Deity of Christ, the Person and work of the Spirit, the value of Christ's work on the cross, and future retribution. It teaches that it is possible for those who have died to communicate, through a medium, with those who are living. This is not something new. This cult has been in existence for at least 4,000 years (Deuteronomy 18:9-13). It is *strictly forbidden* by God (Exodus 22:18; Leviticus 19:26-31; Deuteronomy 18:9; Isaiah 8:19). Its resurgence is one of the signs of the "perilous times" (1 Timothy 4:1-2, RV) of the last days. Despite the fact that much trickery is involved in spiritist seances, undoubtedly communications are received from the spirit world. However, these are not messages from those who have died, but are really communications from demons who impersonate them. The Bible makes it clear that the spirits of departed ones have no communication with earth (Luke 16:19-31). Warn faithfully regarding this error for the curse of God attends those who engage in it (1 Chronicles 10:13; 2 Kings 21:2-12). Seek to lead such a one to see his sin and repent and turn to the Lord.

Mormonism

There are two groups of Mormons—the Church of Jesus Christ of Latter Day Saints with headquarters in Salt Lake City, Utah, and the Reorganized Church with headquarters in Independence, Missouri. Most Mormons you meet are the former. The cult is expanding rapidly. Its active missionaries are, for the most part, clean-cut, well-groomed, intelligent young people who devote two years of their lives to missionary work. Their religion is one of practical good works. Its educational, social, cultural and religious activities are highly organized and church centered. Mormonism is a force to be reckoned with.

Most Mormons have been taught a whitewashed version of the highly unsavory history of their church. The cult was founded by a shiftless ne'er-do-well named Joseph Smith, a young man whose chief interest seemed to be that of treasure hunting. He made the ludicrous claim that an angel named Moroni appeared at his bedside in 1823 and commissioned him to receive a new revelation from God. He subsequently revealed to Smith the location of some hidden golden plates containing a lengthy message inscribed in "reformed Egyptian" (a nonexistent language). With the aid of some magic spectacles (called the Urim and Thummim by Joseph Smith) the "prophet" was able to translate the text into King James English complete with any number of grammatical and historical errors. Thoughtful Mormon scribes have sought to expunge the worst of the blunders from this "translation" to make it palatable for a more sophisticated age. The resulting work is known as *The Book of Mormon*. To this the Mormons have added two other works, *Doctrine and Covenant* and *The Pearl of Great Price*. These three books are placed on a par with the Bible as inspired revelations.

The Mormons claim that the Bible predicts the giving of the *Book of Mormon*, that the *Book of Mormon* interprets the Old Testament and that it is part of a new covenant with Israel. Yet it clashes with the Biblical revelation in numerous ways and its tales of great extinct civilizations bring the cult into conflict with modern archaeology and anthropology. The *Book of Mormon* also contains a number of obvious plagiarisms from the King James Version of the Bible (!) and a number of false prophecies. It is now generally believed that much of the *Book of Mormon* was lifted wholesale from the fiction of Solomon Spaulding, a retired minister who wrote romances with a Biblical flavor.

The early history of Mormonism is interesting since it sheds much light on the shady origins of the cult. It is a stormy history. Mormons were vigorously persecuted for their heretical and immoral doctrines, polygamy originally being one of the main planks in the cult's platform. Joseph Smith was eventually assassinated but not before he had received 135 allegedly direct revelations from God including a revelation to institute polygamy.

The mantle of Smith fell on Brigham Young, a clever and courageous man given to fits of ruthlessness and one of the giants of the cult. It was under Brigham Young that the cultists began their great trek to the valley of the great Salt Lake in what is now the state of Utah. Young ruled the church with an iron hand for more than thirty years. Each succeeding president of the Mormon church claims infallible apostolic succession from Joseph Smith.

Mormon doctrine is a mixture of error. Mormons claim that their priesthood is divinely appointed, being a continuation of both the Aaronic and Melchizedek priesthoods. This priesthood embraces church presidents, apostles, high priests, elders and office holders and ultimately takes in every male member of the church above the age of twelve. Hebrews 7 teaches that the one Melchizedek Priest today is the Lord Jesus and that He has abolished the Aaronic priesthood. Moreover according to 1 Peter 2:9-10 and Revelation 1:4-6 all believers are priests. Ours is a spiritual priesthood and has need of none of the trappings of a mere religion.

The Mormon doctrine of God is polytheistic and pagan. God is an exalted man; the universe is habited by different gods who procreate spirit children who are then embodied on various planets. God Himself has a body of flesh and bone. The Bible teaches that God is a Spirit (John 4:24). The God of the Mormons is not the God of the Bible.

The doctrine of the virgin birth is garbled by the Mormons. Brigham Young taught that Jesus was the offspring of a mortal mother and an immortal, resurrected and glorified Father. The Lord Jesus was thus not "conceived of the Holy Ghost" as the Bible teaches (Luke 1:35).

Mormon doctrine of salvation involves faith in their Christ and also baptism by immersion, obedience to the dogmas of the Mormon church, good works and keeping the commandments of God. This is in contrast with many Scriptures which teach that salvation is "not of works." Mormons teach that all men will ultimately be saved in contrast with Matthew 25:41, 46; Revelation 19:19–21:11.

The Jew

Very many Jews have been led to accept Christ as their Messiah and Savior. A good working knowledge of the Old Testament is essential. There are certain basic truths to show to the Jew.

1. Old Testament Prophecies Have Been Fulfilled in Christ

He is the promised Messiah; seed of Abram (Genesis 12:2-3); of Judah (Genesis 49:10; Micah 5:2); of David (Isaiah 11:1-10; Jeremiah 23:5-6). He was to be born of a virgin (Isaiah 7:14) in Bethlehem (Micah 5:2). His rejection (Psalm 22; Isaiah 53) and His return (Zechariah 12:10) are both foretold.

2. Old Testament Sacrifices and Types Have Been Fulfilled in Christ

Study Leviticus 17:11, compare Hebrews 9:18-28. Show that the Passover has been fulfilled in Christ (Exodus 12; John 1:29, etc.). To the objection of the Trinity show Genesis 1:1. The word "God" here is a plural word meaning more than two (compare Genesis 1:26).

3. Warn of the Danger of Rejecting Christ

Study Hebrews 10:26-29. Make yourself especially familiar with the Epistle to the Hebrews if you would deal with Jews.

Church Members

Because of its impact over the centuries and in the world today, we need to take a special look at Catholicism.

Thousands of Roman Catholics have been won into the clear light and liberty of the glorious gospel of Christ. Remember that the Roman Catholic Church holds and teaches some fundamental truths, such as the Deity of Christ, His virgin birth, sinless life, wonderful miracles, His substitutionary death, His resurrection and ascension. They also believe in the inspiration of the Scriptures. We praise God for their preservation of these truths over the centuries. The trouble is they have mixed so much superstition, paganism, and error with the truth that its adherents are blinded to the soul-emancipating gospel.

When dealing with a Roman Catholic, use a version which is acceptable to him. Nowadays many Catholics will accept a *King James* Bible. At any rate the *Confraternity New Testament* is excellent. If need be use the *Douay Version* which is very similar to the Authorized Version except in the footnotes which the Roman Catholic regards as equally inspired. Do not attack the Catholic Church or defend Protestantism. The Catholics have been taught a different history of the Church than have Protestants. Their view on the Reformation is totally distinct from ours so avoid arguments on the subject. Don't dwell on the sins of the Roman Catholic clergy. Your object is not to unload your opinion of the Catholic Church but to win a soul for Christ.

Many Roman Catholics when approached will say they are Christians. Do not contradict them but show that a Christian is warranted to *know* from the Word of God that his sins are forgiven; that he has peace with God; that he is the possessor of eternal life; that he is sure of heaven. By this means he may be convicted of the falsity of his own claim to be a Christian.

Briefly, the Roman Catholic Church denies the sole Mediatorship of Christ, and adds Mary, the saints and the clergy. It denies the assurance of salvation, justification by faith alone, apart from works and the sole authority of the Scriptures. It classes the writings of the early fathers, and edicts of the Pope, as of equal authority.

There are at least five good methods of approach to the Roman Catholic:

1. On the Ground of the Assurance of Salvation

Show it is possible for a person to know he is saved. He can know his sins are all forgiven (Acts 10:43; 13:38-39; Ephesians 1:7; 1 John 1:9; Colossians 2:13); that he has eternal life *now* (1 John 5:13; John 3:16, 36; 5:24). In 1 John "know" occurs 36 times. He can know this assurance is possible to all who believe, and not to a privileged few (John 1:12; 20:31; 2 Timothy 1:12; Revelation 22:17).

2. On the Ground of the New Birth

Show that it is possible to be religious, and not be a Christian. Nicodemus (John 3) had been circumcised and had identified himself with the Jewish faith but was yet unsaved. Show that baptism and regeneration are distinct in Scripture. The thief was saved, but not baptized (Luke 23:43); Simon

Magus was baptized, but not regenerated (Acts 8:9-24). Show that the new birth is the work of the Spirit of God applying the Word of God (John 3:8); that He imparts a new nature (2 Peter 1:4) and seals the believing sinner (John 3:14-16; Ephesians 1:13), thus producing a new creation (2 Corinthians 5:17), evidenced by a new life (Titus 2:11-12; Romans 12:1-2; James 1:27; 1 Peter 1:23).

3. On the Ground of One Mediator

Show that men are instructed to pray to God alone through Christ (John 14:6; 15:16; 16:23-24); that Christ alone is the Mediator (1 Timothy 2:5; Acts 4:12; 1 John 2:1); that Peter and Paul and John resented undue reverence being paid them (Acts 10:25-26; 14:8-16; Revelation 19:10; 22:8-9); that Mary put Christ first (John 2:5). Notice her advice and apply her words. Show that Christ put her on the same footing as the disciples (Matthew 12:46-50; Luke 11:27-28; compare John 2:4; 19:26-27); that Mary confessed her need of a Savior and took her place before God as a sinner (Luke 1:46-47; 2:21-24). After Acts 1:14 her name is never mentioned again. True, she is "blessed," but only because of the One born of her (Luke 1:28-55). Note in verse 47 Mary said, "My Savior."

4. On the Ground of Justification by Faith Alone

Study Romans 3:24-28; 4:5; Galatians 2:16; 3:10-13; Ephesians 2:8-10. Show the difference between salvation "by works," and "unto good works," or "with a view to good works."

5. On the Ground of the Word of God Alone

Urge the Roman Catholic to read it for himself. It will bring light (Psalm 119:130; Hebrews 4:12-13; James 1:18). If he hasn't a Bible give him one and advise him to read John's Gospel. Keep in touch with him, pray for him, and you may have the joy of winning him for Christ.

Ministering to Prisoners

In view of an increasing concern to win prisoners to Christ we include guidelines for ministering to them.

1. Don't come across with a self-righteous or "better than thou" attitude.

2. Go slow! Learn to listen and hear a man out before addressing his needs. They often need to "unload" their fears and frustrations before they can hear what you have to say.
3. Don't give any false promises—salvation will not guarantee their physical freedom or even their personal safety while incarcerated. It will bring forgiveness, new attitudes, a new life.
4. Don't get side-tracked with secondary issues—the justice system, capital punishment, etc.—rather draw their attention to their personal accountability before God and what He offers in His Son.
5. Don't express disgust or personal revulsion because of the nature of their crime. We are all capable of any sin and had we been in their situation may very well have fallen to the same temptation.
6. Don't be put off by their gruffness and apparent hardness. Most often this is just a "front" to deal with the harshness and possible violence in jail. Within they are crying out for truth.
7. Don't give up because they may not seem interested at first—this too is often a false front. Pray for wisdom and discernment to find the words that will "open them up."
8. Emphasize God's love and forgiveness rather than His judgment (in most cases). Inmates are generally people with a very poor self image and are usually quite aware of judgment and punishment already.
9. Emphasize that God wants to make them new creatures with a purpose for living—they are very much in need of hope.
10. Point out Christ's amazing forgiveness clearly. Many feel they can never be forgiven because of the sinful and wicked deeds they have committed. Point out that Moses, David, and Paul were all murderers yet they were forgiven and used by God.
11. Don't let them blame society, the "system" or anything else for their sinful behavior. They must admit that they are responsible for their actions before they can be helped.
12. Be willing to give of yourself as a true friend in helping to meet their legitimate needs. Most have been forsaken by family and associates once they are incarcerated.

13. Don't be naive or easily taken in by stories you hear—expect to be lied to much of the time. Don't allow yourself to be used or taken for granted.
14. Expect to see many false professions and to see many failures and difficulties in dealing with these people. Most are from deeply troubled lives and backgrounds.
15. Don't necessarily press for immediate conversions. Let the truth become understood and let them know the seriousness of the decision they are making. Let the Holy Spirit save people; we can't!

Verses to Memorize

How shall we escape, if we neglect so great salvation; which at the first began to be spoken by the Lord, and was confirmed unto us by them that heard him.	But this man, after he had offered one sacrifice for sins forever, sat down on the right hand of God.
For the word of God is quick, and powerful, and sharper than any two-edged sword, piercing even to the dividing asunder of soul and spirit, and of the joints and marrow, and is a discerner of the thoughts and intents of the heart.	But be ye doers of the word, and not hearers only, deceiving your own selves.
Neither is there any creature that is not manifest in his sight: but all things are naked and opened unto the eyes of him with whom we have to do.	Whereas ye know not what shall be on the morrow. For what is your life? It is even a vapour, that appeareth for a little time, and then vanisheth away.
Wherefore he is able also to save them to the uttermost that come unto God by him, seeing he ever liveth to make intercession for them.	Therefore to him that knoweth to do good, and doeth it not, to him it is sin.

Hebrews 10:12	Hebrews 2:3
James 1:22	Hebrews 4:12
James 4:14	Hebrews 4:13
James 4:17	Hebrews 7:25

Chapter 11

The Objector and the Skeptic

The Objector

This person's objections rise from many sources. Most of them are common, and all can be answered from the Bible.

1. Objections Relating to the Bible and Its Doctrines

"The Bible is full of contradictions." Hand the objector your Bible and ask him to show you one. Usually he cannot do so, but be prepared if they show you an apparent one. (*Errors and Contradictions in the Bible* by R. A. Torrey is a good book to study in order to equip yourself to handle many common objections of this type.) Now show him how absurd it is to find fault with a book he has never read. Turn him to 1 Corinthians 2:14; John 3:3, 7, and perhaps 2 Peter 2:12.

"The Bible is an impure book." Ask the objector what he means by impure. Does the Bible excite the reader to impurity of thought, word, or deed, or does it awaken a desire to imitate the deed, or does it stir one's repugnance and disgust at the foul sin it describes? If the latter, then the Bible is the purest of books for this is what it does (Titus 1:15; Psalm 12:6; 2 Peter 2:11-12). A medical book is not at all suitable for public reading, but no one calls it "impure" because of this.

"God is unjust to create men to condemn them." God created man that He might bless him (Genesis 1:28; Psalm 102:18; Revelation 4:11). God does not desire to condemn, but to save humanity, in proof of which He gave His Son who, in turn, gave His life (Mark 10:45; Ezekiel 33:11; John 3:16-17; 2 Peter 3:9). Moreover if a sinner is eternally lost it will be due to his willful rejection of the only remedy and the alone Savior (John 5:40; 2 Thessalonians 2:12; Matthew 25:41).

"There is no such place as hell." Ask the objector, "How do you know? On what authority do you say this?" Christ declared there is a hell and He died and rose, and no one has returned from eternity to contradict Him (Luke 16:19–31; Mark 9:43–48; Matthew 25:46; Revelation 20:11–15)!

"Hell is in this life." This cannot be, for there are no Christians in hell and many Christians are on earth. Remind the objector that no gospel is preached in hell yet he is hearing the gospel; no salvation is offered in hell yet this gift is offered to him. It is true the wicked have no peace in this life, but it will be worse in eternity.

"The Bible is not inspired." Study the Emmaus course *God's Word Is Truth* to arm yourself against this objection. Ask the objector, "What do you mean by inspired?" Probably he can't tell you. Show him that unbelief in a fact doesn't alter its truth (Romans 3:3-4; 2 Timothy 3:15-16; 1 Thessalonians 2:13; 2 Peter 1:20-21; Hebrews 4:12).

"I'm sincere in my belief." This is similar to the claim, "It doesn't matter what a man believes providing he is sincere." The obvious answer to that claim is, "What about the people who accidentally take poison sincerely imagining it to be medicine? Does their sincerity save them?" It is possible for a person to be "sincerely mistaken" and die just as certainly as though he were a suicide. Nicodemus was sincere but needed to be born again (John 3). The rich young man was sincere but lacked one thing (Mark 10:21). Saul was sincere but mistaken (Acts 26:9-11). It is God's Word, and not human ideas, that is the standard.

"A God of love will never punish His creatures." Ask the objector, "How do you know?" God is not only love, but *light* (1 John 1:5). He can never be loving *at the expense* of His holiness, justice, and righteousness. God hates sin and must punish it (Romans 1:18-20; 2:4-5; Exodus 34:6-7; Psalm 11:4-7; Daniel 9:12-14; Deuteronomy 32:4). Show that God in *love* gave His Son (John 3:16) and then, in *light,* visited all His wrath on the One who willingly bore our sins (2 Corinthians 5:21; Matthew 27:46; Isaiah 53:5-6). All who willfully despise, reject, or neglect such a Savior by such an act seal their own eternal doom (John 3:18-19, 36; Hebrews 10:29; Revelation 21:8).

2. Relating to the Inconsistencies of Christians

It is a common objection that there are too many hypocrites. Always admit this but point out that good money is not thrown away because counterfeit money is sometimes found among it. Hypocrisy is foretold and condemned in the Bible (Matthew 23:1-3, 15-33). A person should be careful whom he calls a hypocrite for he may be one himself (Matthew 7:1-5; Romans 2:21-23)! Perhaps the *splinter* a person imagines is in his brother's eye is but the reflection of the *plank* that is in his own! Ask the objector if he is always consistent with his own standard of living or morals. Point out that a person has to be smaller than the hypocrite behind whom he hides. Ask the objector if he wants to be considered a smaller man, morally, than the one he is hiding behind? The fact that a banker kills his wife doesn't prove that all bankers kill their wives! The fact that one who professes to be a Christian is a hypocrite doesn't mean all Christians are such. Consider asking the objector if he wants to spend eternity in the company of these hypocrites? No hypocrite will be in heaven (Matthew 23:33), so he had better get really saved. Show that Christ, and not His faulty followers, is the Object for our trust and example. The Bible doesn't say, "Come to Christians," or "Believe on the church," but urges sinners to come to and trust in Christ (Matthew 11:28; Isaiah 45:22; John 10:9; 14:6).

3. Relating to Personal Difficulties

"I'm not so bad." Ask, "What is the standard for crime—your ideas, or the law of the land?" Show God's standard by which sin is measured. Read Matthew 22:36-40; Luke 10:27-28, now see James 2:10. Ask the objector, "Have you kept this law perfectly and at all times during your lifetime? If not, then you have come short of it and are a guilty sinner (Romans 3:19, 23). It is *God's* estimation of sin and not *yours* that counts in the final analysis."

"I'm doing the best I can." Throw this one right back. Ask, "Are you really? On every occasion in your life have you *always* done your *very* best? Have you never told a lie, harbored an evil and impure thought, committed a wrong deed, or assumed a wrong attitude to God? Can you honestly, as before God, say this? Do you claim to be absolutely perfect? Is it not true that you have often not done your best?" To fail once is to sin and sin demands punishment (Romans 6:23; Ezekiel 18:4). No person is ever "doing his best" while rejecting Christ and refusing to repent and believe the gospel. Here is a man on the top story of a burning building. The fireman places a ladder right up to his window and shouts, "Climb down," but this man is too busy doing his best to make a ladder of his own by which to save himself. That man's "best" is his "worst"! The best thing for that man to do is to cease his own efforts, and trust to the ladder that has been provided (Ephesians 2:8-9; Romans 4:5).

"I can't believe." Always counter that with the question, *"Who* can't you believe? Is God's Word untrustworthy? Do you believe what man says? See 1 John 5:9-10. Would you make God a liar? To doubt God is an insult to Him." Point out it would be more honest to say, "I *won't* believe."

"There are so many religions." Admit this but point out that there is only one Savior, and only one way of salvation. Moreover, Christianity is not a religion, but a Person (John 10:9; 14:6; Acts 4:12; 1 John 5:12). Show how Christianity is centered in a *Person,* whereas religion is centered in a *belief.* Religion didn't die for our sins, doesn't invite sinners, or promise salvation to all who believe; but Christ does all this and really saves all who trust Him.

"The Christian life is too difficult." The answer to this is that it is not only difficult, but impossible for anyone to live in his own power. But Christ gives the power to live the life (John 1:12; Romans 1:16; Matthew 11:28-30; Isaiah 14:3). The Christian life is not an easy one. No man can *start* the Christian life until he has *the Christian life* to *start* with; Christ gives that life (John 1:4, 12-13; 4:14; 5:24). Show that the sinner's path is even harder (Proverbs 13:15; Isaiah 57:20-21), and his doom sure (1 Peter 4:17).

"There is too much to give up." Ask, "What if you lose your soul (Mark 8:36)? Will the pleasures of this world compensate you for your eternal loss?" It is a question of profit and loss (Romans 6:23). Show it is not a case of "giving up" something but of receiving Someone and something far better: Christ and salvation with its joy, peace, and satisfaction (John 14:1-3; 15:11; Philippians 1:6; 3:9; 1 Thessalonians 5:23-24; Ephesians 1:3, 7; Romans 15:13). Did you ever hear of anyone regretting he had trusted Christ (Mark 10:22)? What did he lose?

"I'm a church member." Use many of the same points covered in chapter ten. Point out the necessity of the new birth (John 3).

"I'm too bad." One seldom hears this. Agree with the person and tell him he's far worse than he can imagine, but not beyond the reach of salvation (Isaiah 1:18; 1 John 1:7; 1 Timothy 1:15; Hebrews 7:25; Luke 19:10; Acts 13:38-39).

"My friends will laugh at me." Agree to that but show it is better to have one's friends laugh than God! (Proverbs 1:24-30). It is better to face men's rejection than Christ's rejection (Mark 8:38; Matthew 10:32-33). Warn of the fear of man (John 12:42-43; Proverbs 29:25; Isaiah 51:7; Matthew 10:28).

The Skeptic

1. Classes of Skeptics

There is *the skeptic* who doubts the fundamental doctrines of Christianity and questions the Scriptures as the only rule of faith and practice. There is *the unbeliever* who rejects the tenets of Christianity. There is *the infidel* who opposes as well as rejects the truth of God's Word. "Infidelity" is the opposite of "fidelity," and has the thought of being untrue and faithless. There is *the deist* who admits there is a God, but denies that the Scriptures contain a revelation from Him. There is *the agnostic* who denies that anyone knows, or can know, whether or not there is a God. There is *the freethinker* who refuses to permit his thought to become "biased" by authority or dogma and particularly by Christian authority and dogma.

2. The Dishonest Skeptic

This person's professed skepticism is a mere covering for continuation in a life of sin and a slave to his conscience. When dealing with such, probe deeply and deeply ingrained sin will be disclosed. Do not argue with this kind of person for this is what he wants. Soltau says, "Never try to prove anything to a skeptic, for evidence is of no value to such a man." Listen to what he has to say and then quote a Scripture calculated to sting the conscience and arouse him to a sense of sin and folly (1 Corinthians 1:18; 3:18; 2 Corinthians 4:3-4; Hebrews 9:27; Psalm 14:1; Mark 16:16). Use the "sword" on him and keep on quoting nothing but Scripture and pray it may cut him to the heart.

3. The Sincere Skeptic

The difficulty with this class is their inability to believe. Find out by questioning what the person thinks *believing* is. Then show that the faith he is called upon to exercise in God and His Word is similar to the faith he uses daily in his business, social, and domestic life. The difference is not in the *nature,* but in the *object* of that faith. Show that to believe a person is to accept what he says as true simply because of the character of the one who makes the statement. Now use 1 John 5:9-10. Then show what God has said concerning sin (1 John 1:8-10; Romans 3:9-23) and its consequences (John 3:18-19, 36), about God's love (John 3:16; Romans 5:6-8) and Christ's work (2 Corinthians 5:21; 1 Peter 2:24); point out the way and assurance of salvation (John 5:24; 1 John 5:13). Show that this is what God asks him to believe. Is *God* trustworthy? Will *He* fulfill His promise? Here you may give your own testimony to God's saving grace.

A. T. Pierson suggests this method of dealing with the serious skeptic. Tell him to *search the Scriptures* (John 5:39). Challenge him to read John's Gospel for himself. The Scriptures bear their own mark of inspiration (John 20:31). Suggest he *pray in secret for light* (Matthew 6:6). God will not discourage any sincere effort to draw near to Him (Acts 17:27; Hebrews 11:6). Urge him to *put into practice what he learns* (John 7:17). Act up to the light He gives and you will have more light (Hosea 6:3). *When convinced, he can come to Christ* and He will give rest (Matthew 11:28-30). A. T. Pierson declared he had never known this method to fail.

Dr. R. A. Torrey's method consisted in asking questions. *What can't you believe?* Get as full an answer as possible to provide a starting place. *Why can't you believe?* This may prove to be an eye-opener and show how groundless are his reasons for unbelief. Ask, "Do you believe there is a God?" If he answers, "No," ask, "Do you believe in prayer?" "No." "Do you believe in any part of anything in the Bible?" If he still answers, "No," ask, "Do you believe there is an absolute difference between right and wrong?" If he says, "Yes," then inquire, *"Do you live up to what you believe?"* Here is the real crux of his difficulty. Use John 7:17; Hosea 6:3. Show him that the Lord makes a fair proposition in these verses: that if a man will *do* His will as far as he knows it, he will be brought to *know,* and thus be brought from skepticism to faith.

Torrey would then draw out a written statement and ask him to sign it. The statement read, "I believe there is an absolute difference between right and wrong. I hereby take my stand upon the right to follow it wherever it carries me. I promise to make an honest search to find out if Jesus Christ is the Son of God. If I find that He is, I promise to accept Him as my Savior, and confess Him as my Lord before the world." Then read him John 20:31 and get him to pledge himself to read a portion of the Gospel of John each day. Many have been led into the light this way.

Verses to Memorize

Forasmuch as ye know that ye were not redeemed with corruptible things, as silver and gold, from your vain conversation received by tradition from your fathers; But with the precious blood of Christ, as of a lamb without blemish and without spot.	The Lord is not slack concerning his promise, as some men count slackness; but is longsuffering to us-ward, not willing that any should perish, but that all should come to repentance.
Who his own self bare our sins in his own body on the tree, that we, being dead to sins, should live unto righteousness: by whose stripes ye were healed.	If we say that we have no sin, we deceive ourselves, and the truth is not in us. If we confess our sins, he is faithful and just to forgive us our sins, and to cleanse us from all unrighteousness.
For the time is come that judgment must begin at the house of God: and if it first begin at us, what shall the end be of them that obey not the gospel of God? And if the righteous scarcely be saved, where shall the ungodly and the sinner appear?	My little children, these things write I unto you, that ye sin not. And if any man sin, we have an advocate with the Father, Jesus Christ the righteous: And he is the propitiation for our sins: and not for ours only, but also for the sins of the whole world.
We have also a more sure word of prophecy; whereunto ye do well that ye take heed, as unto a light that shineth in a dark place, until the day dawn, and the day star arise in your hearts.	Love not the world, neither the things that are in the world. If any man love the world, the love of the Father is not in him. For all that is in the world, the lust of the flesh, and the lust of the eyes, and the pride of life, is not of the Father, but is of the world.

2 Peter 3:9	1 Peter 1:18-19
1 John 1:8-9	1 Peter 2:24
1 John 2:1-2	1 Peter 4:14, 18
1 John 2:15-16	2 Peter 1:19

Chapter 12

More Types to Deal With

The Excuser

This person is similar to the objector, but his excuses are obviously shallow. He is usually flippant, his excuses hackneyed and outworn. Show him that excuses are not new. Warn that God might accept his excuse and excuse him from being saved and being in heaven (Luke 14:24). Here are some typical excuses.

"I'm as good as any church member." This is not saying much, for very many of them have never been born again. In any case, so-called church members are not the standard of God's acceptance but the new birth. Apply John 3:3, 5, and compare Romans 3:10-19. "To be no worse is to be no better."

"There's plenty of time." God has only one time in which He is prepared to save (2 Corinthians 6:2; Hebrews 3:7-8). Point out he cannot be saved when he likes, but only when God likes and God's time is *now*.

"I'll turn over a new leaf." What about the sins recorded on the old pages of the book? Does turning over a new leaf pay the old debts in a businessman's account book? God requires that which is past (Ecclesiastes 3:15). Point out man's inability to change self (Jeremiah 13:23; James 2:10). Ask, "What will you do when you come to the end of the book and have no more leaves to turn?"

"I'll take my chance with the rest." God's Word doesn't speak of *chances*, but of *certainties*. There's no *chance* of being eternally lost if you die in your sins—it's a *certainty*. Point out your *chance* is your *choice*. People don't take "chances" when they jump from a ten-story building or stand in front of a moving locomotive. Give this person 1 Thessalonians 5:3; Hebrews 2:3; 10:27; John 8:21.

The Ignorant

Use the same approach as for the careless and indifferent. Present their need and God's remedy as simply as possible.

The Anxious

How good it is to meet such and what a joy to take the Word of God and use it to lead them to put their trust in Christ and enter into the assurance of their salvation! Use the method found in lesson nine from the division *Point to Christ.* Dr. Campbell Morgan suggests that three questions be put to this kind of person. Are you willing to be saved? Are you willing to be saved in God's way and on God's terms? If I can show you God's way and His terms, are you willing to be saved *now?* This throws the matter entirely on the inquirer and clears the field for action.

The Confused

This is a fairly common type. These people are anxious to be saved but have real difficulties in grasping the truth of the gospel. They express their confusion in various ways.

"I haven't enough faith." It is not faith that saves, but Christ (Ephesians 2:8). It is *"through"* faith not *"by"* faith (Mark 5:27-28). A man has great faith in a weak bank and puts all his money in it; but the bank fails and he loses all his money. Another man has a little faith in a strong bank, puts his money in it, and it stands. What made his money safe—his *faith* or the *bank?* Christ is the Object of faith and whether your faith is weak or strong, He saves all who trust their souls to Him (Mark 9:23-24). It is not the *amount* of faith that saves but the *Object,* Christ, who saves (John 6:37).

"I've tried to believe and cannot." Ask, "Would you say this to your mother if she told you something?" It would be an insult to suggest you couldn't, or wouldn't, accept her word (1 John 5:10). This type of person is trying to believe in his believing and not in Christ. A ship's anchor is thrown *overboard,* and not *inside* the ship, when the captain wishes it to be at rest. We must not anchor in ourselves, but in Christ. Offer this type of person a tract and when he accepts it, ask, "Did you 'try' to take it, or did

you *take* it without trying? You were occupied with the *gift* and not with the *means* by which you received the gift. Forget your believing and look to Christ. The emphasis is not on 'believe' but on 'Christ.'"

"I've always believed." This cannot be, for if so, then the person has always been saved and, if always saved, then he has never been lost. Christ only came to seek and save the lost (Luke 19:10). Point out the difference between believing *about* and believing *in*. Say, "Suppose you were taken seriously ill. You have heard and believed about two doctors who live near you. You say to your wife, 'Send for Dr. Smith.' Your wife replies, 'But what about Dr. Brown?' You reply, 'I believe about them both that they are doctors, but I believe *in* Dr. Smith, so send for him.'" Most people believe *about* Christ, but not so many have believed *in* Him by *committing themselves* to him for salvation (2 Timothy 1:12).

"I have no feelings." Show the Divine order to be first *fact,* then *faith,* then *feeling*. To reverse the order brings confusion. A person must accept the fact of his lost condition and Christ's finished work. If he puts his faith in Christ as his own personal Savior the feelings will come, sooner or later. Note in Luke 17:14 it was "as they went" that the feeling came. The lepers acted in faith even though they did not realize their leprosy was gone. When they did so, the feelings came. There is no such thing as "feeling saved," but there is such a thing as feeling glad because of the knowledge of one's salvation. Apply John 5:24; 1 John 5:13.

"I'm afraid I have committed the unpardonable sin." This excuse is a sure indication the person hasn't committed this sin for those who do will have no further anxiety of soul. Point out what this sin is (Matthew 12:31-32). It is the deliberate and *willful* attributing to the Devil the work of the Spirit of God. Show this person that the very fact of his being concerned about salvation is due to the Spirit's work and proves he has not committed this sin. Then turn him to John 6:37; 1 Timothy 1:15; 2 Peter 3:9.

"I don't know if I am one of the elect." This is seldom heard but it is good to be ready. Show that election has nothing to do with the sinner. It is a truth only for those who are saved. Ask this person if he would be justified in reading a letter not addressed to him? Show him to whom the epistles are written (Ephesians 1:1, 4-5; 1 Thessalonians 1:1-4; 1 Peter 1:1, 23). Now turn him to the gospel whose invitation is "whosoever will" (John 3:16; 6:37; Acts 10:43; Romans 10:9-13).

"I've tried to make myself believe I am saved, and I cannot." There is a very good reason for this. People are not saved by trying to make themselves believe they are saved. "The Bible doesn't say, "Believe you are saved, and you are saved," but, "Believe on the Lord Jesus Christ and thou shalt be saved" (Acts 16:31). A person might just as well say, "Believe you are the President of the United States and you are the President!" What you and I believe is a small thing. It is what God's Word says that counts. What does He say? Apply Romans 10:9-10; Acts 13:38, etc.

"I'm afraid I won't be able to hold on." Salvation and security are not conditioned by a person's "holding on to Christ," but by His holding on to him! Apply John 10:27-30; Romans 14:4. Take out a pencil and ask, "Can this pencil stand upright on its point?" The answer is obviously "No." Now hold the top of the pencil so that it is upright. Probably he will say, "But you are holding it!" Reply, "Certainly, and that's the only way *you* can stand! Someone must hold you" (Hebrews 7:25).

"How will I know when I am saved?" The answer is, when God tells a person so in His Word. When is that? When that person, as a guilty, lost sinner, believes Christ died for his sins and trusts Him as Savior. Ask, "Who would you rather have inform you that you are saved, God or me?" He will reply, "God." Then show him what God says about those who believe on His Son (1 Corinthians 6:11). Note the "are's." Apply 1 John 5:13; Acts 16:31; John 3:16.

"What about any sins I may commit after I am saved?" Ask, "How many of your sins were *future* when Christ died for them?" The answer is "All of them." Apply 1 John 1:7; Acts 13:38-39. Explain what justification means.

"It's too late." The fact that a person is still alive, and not in hell, proves it is not too late (Deuteronomy 4:30-31). Consider the dying thief (Luke 23, compare John 6:37).

The Backslider

The word is used in the Old Testament but the fact of it is seen in the New Testament. It has various meanings. It has to do with *inclination*, or *bent* away from God (Proverbs 14:14). As illustrations see Exodus 16:3; Numbers 11:4-6. It means *to go back* as a deliberate act (Jeremiah 2:19; 3:6, 8, 12; 5:6). It means *to turn around* (Hosea 4:16); *to be beguiled*, or to be deceived, and led astray (Jeremiah 3:14, 22; 31:32; 49:4). For examples see David, Jonah, Solomon. In the New Testament, where the word is not used, the thought is clearly seen (Galatians 5:4; 2 Timothy 4:10; 1 Corinthians 5:1, 5; 9:27). As an illustration see Peter's denial in Mark 14:54, 66-72. Study the steps that led to this denial. Other examples are John Mark (Acts 13:13; 15:37-38; compare 2 Timothy 4:11); the church at Ephesus (Revelation 2:4). That it is possible for a Christian to lose his joy, assurance, and usefulness, is clear from the Scriptures. There are various types of backsliders. There are *imitation Christians*—those who mistakenly imagine they are backsliders, but who have never really been born again. They say, "I've tried before and failed." These must be shown kindly, and as a result of careful questioning, that they were never real Christians. Consequently, they need to be saved. Ask them to give you an account of their conversion and let them talk themselves out. It will soon be seen where they are spiritually. Then deal with them as unsaved persons.

There are *careless backsliders*—those who have drifted away and seem unconcerned about the whole matter. These need a jolt to startle them out of their complacency. You could use Romans 2:4-5; Jonah 1:6; Jeremiah 2:5, 13, 19; 1 Kings 11:9. Point out to such a person that his backslidden condition is an impeachment of Christ's keeping and satisfying power and that he is an advertisement, to the unsaved, of the folly of becoming a Christian. Show that he is a stumbling block in the way of the spiritually dead who use him as an encouragement to live in their sins (Ephesians 5:14; 4:17-25). Drive home the truth that the only proof he can give that he is a genuine backslider is by returning in repentance, confession, and self-judgment as did the Prodigal (Luke 15).

There are *repentant backsliders*—those who are tired of their wandering and waywardness and now are anxious to return. Seek by questioning to discover the cause of their backsliding. Point out *the sinfulness* of this person's departure from God (Jeremiah 2:5) and *the abysmal folly* of it (Jeremiah 2:13). Show how *essential* to his *restoration* is *true* heart repentance (Revelation 2:4-5). Point out the need for honest and frank confession of sin to God (Jeremiah 14:7; Hosea 14:1-2; 1 John 1:9; Psalm 51), and the need for a deliberate turning from that sin in self judgment (Isaiah 55:7; 1 Corinthians 11:30-33). Get him to *read* some of *God's promises* to the backslider (Isaiah 44:20-22; Jeremiah 3:12-14, 22; 6:16; 24:7; Hosea 2:14-16; 11:8; 2 Corinthians 7:10; Luke 15:11-24). Show the *necessity of restitution,* if he has wronged others. Urge the *necessity for Bible study,* prayer, the fellowship of God's people and service for Him, if they are to go on for God (2 Timothy 2:15; Philippians 4:6-8; Hebrews 10:25; John 21:15-17; Isaiah 40:31).

The Discouraged Christian

How many such there are who long for the encouragement of their fellow believers (Malachi 3:16-17). Let us by God's grace be helpers of one another as opportunity presents itself (Galatians 6:1-4).

The Rewards of Personal Evangelism

In conclusion, consider the rewards of personal evangelism. There is the *joy* that comes from obedience to Christ's commission, and of seeing precious souls saved through our instrumentality (Psalm 126:6; John 13:17; Acts 20:24; 2 John 4, Philippians 4:1). This, in itself, is sufficient reward.

There is the *blessing* it brings into the lives of those we have been used to lead to Christ and who, in turn, will lead others to Him (Genesis 12:2-3). We have been blessed by God that we might be a blessing to others (James 5:20; 1 Corinthians 4:15; 9:16-23).

There is the *commendation of the Lord* Himself. Surely His "well done" will amply compensate for all the toil of the way (Matthew 25:14-23; Luke 19:12-17; Daniel 12:3).

There is the *crown* given by Him. Five crowns are spoken of in Scripture. There is *the crown of rejoicing*. This is the soul winner's crown (1 Thessalonians 2:19-20). There is *the crown of righteousness*. This is the warrior's crown (2 Timothy 4:6-8). There is *the crown of life*. This is the endurer's crown (James 1:12). There is *the crown of glory*. This is the shepherd's or overseer's crown (1 Peter 5:2-4). There is *the incorruptible crown*. This is the faithful runner's crown (1 Corinthians 9:24-27).

Make sure that no man takes your crown.

Verses to Memorize

Herein is love, not that we loved God, but that he loved us, and sent his Son to be the propitiation for our sins.	The same shall drink of the wine of the wrath of God, which is poured out without mixture into the cup of his indignation; and he shall be tormented with fire and brimstone in the presence of the holy angels, and in the presence of the Lamb.
These things have I written unto you that believe on the name of the Son of God; that ye may know that ye have eternal life, and that ye may believe on the name of the Son of God.	And whosoever was not found written in the book of life was cast into the lake of fire.
Now unto him that is able to keep you from falling, and to present you faultless before the presence of his glory with exceeding joy.	But the fearful, and unbelieving, and the abominable, and murderers, and whoremongers, and sorcerers, and idolaters, and all liars, shall have their part in the lake which burneth with fire and brimstone: which is the second death.
Behold, I stand at the door, and knock: if any man hear my voice, and open the door, I will come in to him, and will sup with him, and he with me.	And the Spirit and the bride say, Come. And let him that heareth say, Come. And let him that is athirst come. And whosoever will, let him take the water of life freely.

Revelation 14:10	1 John 4:10
Revelation 20:15	John 5:13
Revelation 21:8	Jude 24
Revelation 22:17	Revelation 3:20

For those who know Christ as Savior, it should be our delight to meet with Him, as He requested, at the Lord's Supper. But does boredom, apathy, uncomfortable silence or even mindless ritual ever encroach upon what should be the highlight of our week?

Join A.P. Gibbs as he leads you to discover hidden treasures in this simple remembrance feast. As you learn, your soul will be refreshed and your praise will overflow from a heart retouched by the Savior.

A great deal of confusion exists in Christendom as to just what constitutes worship. Many Christians put the emphasis of their lives on service for God. Others swing to the other extreme, stressing only the importance of worship.

In His reply to Satan's temptation, Jesus said: "Thou shalt worship the Lord thy God and Him only shalt thou serve." (Matt. 4:10) That quality of worship which does not result in service and that service which does not flow from worship, both come short of the Divine ideal.

Call or go online for more information:
563-585-2070 ♦ www.ecsministries.org

There can surely be no question as to the tremendous importance for the prayerful preparation and effective presentation of the gospel message. With the object of aiding Christians to fulfill this divinely given task, this book has been written.

This books brings Gibb's knowledge of preaching within our reach. His seriousness, thoroughness, energy, and urgency are evident throughout this book. The illustrations of the various types of sermons are especially helpful.

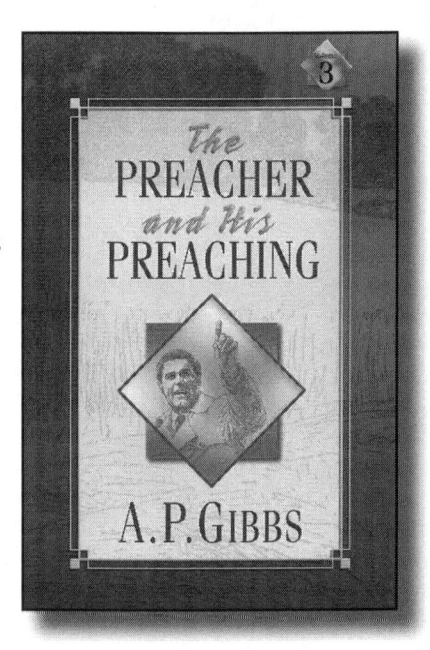

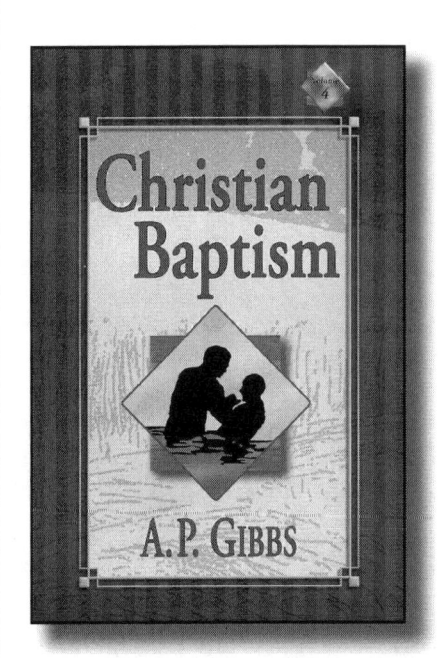

There is much confusion about the meaning of baptism and about how and when an individual should be baptized. This comprehensive and clear study by A. P. Gibbs takes us back to the Bible to help us understand the true significance of baptism and answer the many questions that surround this subject.

A detailed Table of Contents will aid the reader to view the subject as a whole, and also enable him to turn to any part of the subject in which he is particularly interested.

Call or go online for more information:
563-585-2070 ♦ www.ecsministries.org

About the Author

Alfred P. Gibbs (1890–1967) was a noted writer, teacher, and lecturer. He served as a Chaplain in the armed forces in the South Pacific. He eventually attended Moody Bible Institute and was later commended to the Lord's work from a chapel in the Chicago area. During this time, he also served as a visiting instructor at Emmaus Bible College. Mr. Gibbs wrote several texts on teaching and preaching, and composed numerous hymns and choruses.

◆

Resources by A. P. Gibbs

A Dreamer & His Dream

An Introduction to a Study of Church Truth

Child Evangelism

Choice Hymns of the Faith

Christian Baptism

God's Good News

Hymns of Truth and Praise

Hymns of Worship and Remembrance

Personal Evangelism

Preach the Word

The Preacher and His Preaching

The Lord's Supper

Through the Scriptures

Worship: The Christian's Highest Occupation

Call or go online for more information:
563-585-2070 ◆ www.ecsministries.org